GOBBLE UP SCIENCE

Fun Activities to Complete and Eat

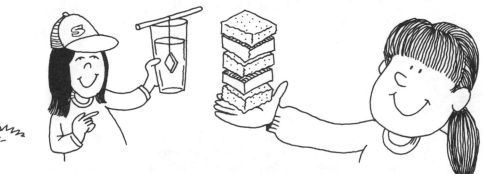

Written by Carol A. Johmann and Elizabeth J. Rieth

Illustrated by Kelly Kennedy

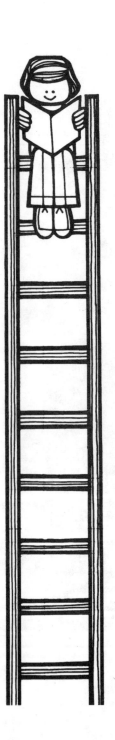

The Learning Works

Cover Design & Illustration:
Kelly Kennedy
Editing:
Jan Stiles & Kim Clark
Page Design & Typesetting:
Clark Editorial & Design

Copyright©1996
The Learning Works, Inc.
P.O. Box 6187
Santa Barbara, California 93160

ISBN: 0-88160-248-5

Contents

Talented Taste Buds

Wacky Water

Contents

(continued)

Contents
(continued)

Colorful Creations

Dynamic Digestion

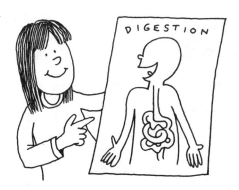

Contents
(continued)

Introduction: What Is *Gobble Up Science*?

What better way for young children to enter the world of science than through their stomachs? In this series of creative activities, children will "gobble up" science as they gobble up nutritious foods and tasty snacks they make themselves.

From examining their sense of taste to learning how they digest food, from working with solutions and reactions to seeing colors in a new light, from fashioning crystals to exploring Earth, children will come away with an understanding of basic science concepts. Along the way, they'll be introduced to and have ample opportunity to practice important problem-solving skills.

By using foods as catalysts for learning, children will:

- create a model of an ice crystal
- predict whether salt makes something sweet even sweeter
- interpret data as they try to keep fruit from turning brown
- observe what it takes to get oil and water to mix
- record data on the chemical reactions that occur in their mouths

Each hands-on activity uses accessible, easy-to-prepare, and, for the most part, healthy foods. The equipment needed can be found in any kitchen. Some activities require adult supervision for cutting fruits and vegetables, using the stove and oven, or helping children through the more involved recipes. These are denoted by the phrase, ◆ adult help. But most activities are designed to be done by the child with minimal adult guidance.

A ☞ suggests an additional activity for kids to do, while a ★ signals an explanation or detailed information, directed mostly toward adults. A ☺ tells students that they can gobble up their creation, while a ☹ indicates that they should not consume the results of that particular experiment.

It's all here, ready for young students to "gobble up." Exploring the world of science has never been more delicious!

A Note to Teachers:
Setting Up a *Gobble Up Science* Center

Learning about science should be an everyday event. There's nothing mysterious or difficult about it. In fact, kids experience science all the time—when they fly a kite, look at the stars, or watch an ant cross the sidewalk.

By providing a place for your students to explore science in the classroom, you'll encourage them to become comfortable manipulating materials and figuring things out for themselves. You'll allow them to develop their problem-solving skills naturally and at their own pace. You'll promote a love of science that will last a lifetime.

Thoughtful planning before setting up a *Gobble Up Science* center will save time later and will allow your students to be as independent as safety considerations permit. Get your children involved by asking them to bring in recyclable containers they can make into bowls and measuring cups. Ask them to bring in old pots and pans, plastic utensils, and nonperishable food supplies. Have them organize the center, labeling shelves and storage containers.

To be most functional, the center needs to have a table or counter and a water supply nearby. Arrangements should be made for using the school's kitchen because some activities require a stove, an oven, a refrigerator, and/or a freezer. Appliances, like electric mixers and blenders, can be brought in as needed. (For an overall list of the supplies needed to carry out the activities, see page 10.)

It is also a good idea to send a letter home with each student in which you ask the parent(s) about any food allergies the student may have.

Be sure to discuss both science and cooking safety. Reproduce and display the poster on page 11, which encourages children to wash their hands before starting each activity. Ask your students to brainstorm their own safety rules for the center. Be sure they include rules for using the stove, oven, and sharp utensils, as well as for cleaning up. Have them design and display a sign listing their rules.

A well-organized and well-stocked *Gobble Up Science* center will provide an exciting place for your students to explore the world of science.

A Note to Parents:
Using *Gobble Up Science* at Home

Science and cooking go hand in hand. Kitchens, after all, are like laboratories. Chemistry is going on all the time, whether you're mixing a salad dressing or relying on baking powder to make a cake rise.

The fun-filled, creative activities presented in *Gobble Up Science* can easily be used to teach science concepts and encourage problem solving in your own kitchen.

Before your child begins a project, go over the instructions with him or her. Be sure your child knows when to ask for help—with handling a sharp knife, for instance, or using the stove. Help your child gather the needed materials. If your child doesn't like a food called for in the activity, be flexible. Substitute cream cheese for peanut butter, for example, or one fruit or vegetable for another.

Encourage your child to answer the questions posed in the activities. Follow up with some of your own. Go through any explanatory material and relate the results of the activity to something else in your child's experience. Encourage your child to extend the learning experience. Could the activity be done in another way? Would reading more about the topic be interesting?

By helping your child "gobble up" science concepts and practice science skills, you'll get across the idea that science is not dull or difficult, but dynamic and doable.

What Supplies Are Needed?

- cutting board (plastic or wooden)
- paring knife (or plastic serrated knife)
- colander
- serving tray
- bowls, plates, cups (paper optional)
- large and small clear glasses
- five-ounce paper and plastic cups
- spoons, forks, knives (plastic optional)
- measuring cups, measuring spoons
- wooden, slotted, and large spoons
- flat and rubber spatulas
- large and small mixing bowls
- large pots, saucepans, frying pans
- cookie sheets, cookie cutters
- baking pan, muffin tin, pie plate
- wire cooling rack
- funnel
- jars with lids
- plastic storage containers
- sealable plastic bags
- plastic wrap, wax paper, aluminum foil
- brown paper bags
- 1/2-gallon milk or juice cartons
- toothpicks, popsicle sticks, straws
- food coloring (red, blue, yellow)

- Epsom salt
- kitchen scales
- popcorn popper (hot-air type recommended)
- blender, juicer (optional)
- electric mixer or rotary beater
- magnifying glass
- prism
- mirror
- window glass
- fishbowl
- flashlight
- eyedroppers, tweezers
- large, round balloons
- blindfold
- cloth handkerchief
- scissors
- white and black paper
- felt-tipped, colored markers
- cardboard, shallow cardboard box
- old magazines and newspapers
- white glue (water soluble)
- masking tape
- ruler
- cotton string
- potting soil and bean seeds
- clean-up materials: liquid detergent, paper towels, sponges, etc.

Don't "gobble up" germs!

Always wash your hands with soap and warm water.

What Is the Food Guide Pyramid?

The Food Guide Pyramid has been recognized as the basic guide for building a healthy diet since its approval by the United States Department of Agriculture in 1992. The pyramid is divided into six major food groups, each with a recommended number of daily servings. This number varies on an individual basis according to age, stage of growth, and activity level.

Serving recommendations have been kept in mind while selecting foods for each activity in *Gobble Up Science*. Foods containing fats and oils have been used minimally, while foods from the bread and cereal and the fruit and vegetable groups have been emphasized. Some experiments require the use of sugars. You may substitute low-fat, fat-free, and sugar-free products unless the fat or sugar content of the food item is vital to the activity. One such example is "Milky Maneuvers" on page 36.

The Food Guide Pyramid is referred to throughout *Gobble Up Science*. It is suggested that a large poster of the pyramid be made for display. This would be a fun kick-off project for children to do at home or school.

Daily servings required in the food pyramid vary according to individual needs at different stages of growth and activity levels.

The Food Guide Pyramid:
A Guide to Daily Food Choices

Fats, Oils, and Sweets
Use sparingly

Milk, Yogurt, and Cheese Group
2–3 servings

Meat, Poultry, Fish, Dry Beans, Eggs, and Nuts Group
2–3 servings

Vegetable Group
3–5 servings

Fruit Group
2–4 servings

Bread, Cereal, Rice, and Pasta Group
6–11 servings

Source: U.S. Department of Agriculture/U.S. Department of Health and Human Services

How Much Is One Serving?

One serving of the bread, cereal, rice, and pasta group is:

- 1 slice of bread,
- 1 ounce of ready-to-eat cereal,
- 1/2 cup of cooked cereal, rice, or pasta, or
- 3–4 small crackers

One serving of the vegetable group is:

- 1 cup of raw, leafy vegetables,
- 1/2 cup of other vegetables, cooked or raw, or
- 3/4 cup of vegetable juice

One serving of the milk, yogurt, and cheese group is:

- 1 cup of milk or yogurt,
- 1¹/₂ ounces of natural cheese, or
- 2 ounces of processed cheese

One serving of the meat, poultry, fish, dry beans, eggs, and nuts group is:

- 2–3 ounces of cooked lean meat, poultry, or fish,
- 1/2 cup of cooked dry beans,
- 1 egg, or
- 2 tablespoons of peanut butter

One serving of the fruit group is:

- 1 medium apple, banana, or orange,
- 1/2 cup of cooked or canned unsweetened fruit, or
- 3/4 cup of fruit juice

Talented Taste Buds

You have about 9,000 of these inside your mouth. What do you think they are?

They're your **taste buds**. They are the organs of taste,
just like your eyes are the organs of sight and your ears are the organs of hearing.

Taste buds are too tiny to see. They're inside the bumps on your tongue.
Even so, you can tell that they are there. How? By tasting!

Your taste buds can sense four basic tastes: sweet, salty, bitter, and sour.
By distinguishing these four tastes, your taste buds help you tell the difference
between all sorts of flavors.

To have a good sense of taste, you must have a good sense of smell.
The look, feel, and texture of foods also play a role in how foods taste.

Your sense of taste helps you decide which foods are fresh and which have gone bad.
Have you ever tasted sour milk? You know in an instant it has turned sour.

Mouth Map

The taste buds on your tongue are grouped according to what they taste.
Can you find the different groups?

What You Need

- teaspoons
- sugar
- salt
- instant coffee granules
- lemon juice
- plate
- mirror
- glass of water

What You Do

1. Put spoonfuls of sugar, salt, coffee, and lemon juice in separate places on a plate.
2. Look in the mirror and stick out your tongue. Wet the tip of your finger and dip it in the sugar. Dab different parts of your tongue with your finger. On the drawing, mark the place where the sugar tastes sweetest.
3. Rinse your mouth and your finger. Repeat Step 2 with salt, coffee, and lemon juice. Rinse in between each item. Be sure to mark on the drawing the places where you tasted salty, bitter, and sour.
4. Find other parts of your mouth that can taste these tastes.

☞ Did you find the groups of taste buds? Sweet is mostly at the tip of your tongue; bitter is mostly at the back. Salty and sour are concentrated along the sides, with salty usually behind sour.

The Nose Knows

Does food taste the same when you have a cold and your nose is all stuffed up?

What You Need

- everything you needed in "Mouth Map" (page 16)

What You Do

1. Repeat the steps in "Mouth Map" on page 16, but this time pinch your nose closed with your thumb and finger while you are testing the sugar, salt, coffee, and lemon juice. Having your nose closed like this is just like having a cold. Mark on the drawing on page 16 the sweet, salty, bitter, and sour taste areas—if you can.

2. Compare your results with your "Mouth Map" results. Could you taste the different tastes as well with your nose closed as you could with it open? _____

   Why? _____

☞ Smear peanut butter on your upper lip and under your nose. Now put a dab of sugar on your tongue while you sniff. What do you taste?

★ *Your sense of smell is important to your sense of taste. If you can't smell your food, you have a hard time tasting it.*

Senses Shutdown

Bet you can't tell the difference between an apple and an onion.
What? You think you can? Let's find out!

What You Need ◆ adult help

- knife and cutting board
- plate
- apple
- potato
- onion
- carrot
- blindfold

Person's Name	Score

What You Do

1. Peel and cut up small bits of apple, potato, onion, and carrot and put them on a plate.
2. Choose a person to do the test. Have the person put on the blindfold and pinch his or her nose shut with thumb and finger. Have the person taste each food and guess what it is. Keep score of the correct guesses. Repeat for everyone who wants to try.

Who was the best taster? _____

Which food was the easiest to identify? _____

Does it matter how food looks and smells? _____

☞ Try testing foods with different textures. That means they feel different on your tongue, like bananas and potato chips. Keep score again. Does texture help people identify foods?

How Sweet It Is

We use lots of things to make foods sweet. We use sugar and honey and maple syrup. Some recipes use corn syrup or molasses. Just how sweet is sweet? Let's find out.

What You Need

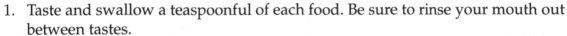

- sugar
- honey
- molasses
- maple syrup
- corn syrup
- teaspoons, one per sweetener for each person tasting
- glass of water

What You Do

1. Taste and swallow a teaspoonful of each food. Be sure to rinse your mouth out between tastes.
2. Rate each food for sweetness compared to the others. Is sugar sweeter than honey? Is maple syrup sweeter than corn syrup? Use 1 for the sweetest, 2 for the next sweetest, and so on.
3. Ask others do this taste test. Record the order of sweetness for each person.

Person's Name	Sugar	Honey	Molasses	Maple	Corn

Sweet or Salty?

What do you think will happen if you put salt on something sweet?
Make a guess before you do this activity. This kind of a guess is called a prediction.

I predict salt will make something sweet taste: ___ salty ___ sweeter ___ the same

What You Need ◆ adult help

- masking tape and marker
- two identical plates
- your favorite sweet melon
- knife and cutting board
- salt
- forks

What You Do

1. Put a piece of masking tape on the bottom of one of the plates so no one can see it.

2. Cut the melon into chunks and put some on both plates.

3. *Lightly* salt the melon that is on the plate with the masking tape.

4. Now shift the plates around so everyone loses track of which one holds the salted melon.

5. Label the plates **A** and **B**. Put the labels where you can see them.

6. Have each person eat a piece of melon from each plate and vote on which piece is sweeter. How many voted for the melon on Plate A? _____ on Plate B? _____

7. Now look at the bottoms of the plates. Which plate has the tape? _____

   Are you surprised? _____ Was your prediction correct? _____

Sweet or Salty?

(continued)

☞ One reason we use salt on foods is to make their flavors seem stronger. Design an experiment to see if salt makes sour foods taste even more sour.

Ask yourself these questions:

• What food do I want to test? _____

• How should I prepare it? _____

• How should I do the test?_____

• What do I predict will happen? _____

Now carry out your experiment and see if your prediction is correct.

Finding Fat

According to the Food Guide Pyramid, you should eat fats and oils only *sparingly*. That means just a little. This activity will help you find out which foods contain fat.

What You Need

- a meal's worth of different foods, including beverages
- brown paper bag
- scissors

What You Do

1. Collect the foods you've decided to test. These could be the foods in your sandwich at lunchtime, the foods being prepared for dinner, or foods you like to snack on.
2. Cut the paper bag into three-inch squares. Label each square with the name of one of the foods you've chosen.
3. Test each solid food by rubbing it with its labeled brown paper square. Test each beverage by dribbling a few drops on its paper square.
4. Let the squares dry, then hold them up to a light. List the squares that the light shines through. These are the foods that contain fat.

_____   _____   _____

_____   _____   _____

★ *Brown paper is made of bits and pieces of wood fibers pressed together, with air in between. This combination of fiber and air reflects and scatters light so much that the light can't pass through. When you rub fat on the paper, the fat replaces the air. The combination of fiber and fat doesn't scatter light as much, so light can pass through the paper.*

Thin or Thick?

One way to reduce fat in your diet is to use nonfat or low-fat milk, yogurt, and cheeses. But some people don't think these products taste as good as the ones with fat.

What You Need

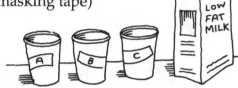

- three identical glasses (labeled **A**, **B**, and **C** with masking tape)
- whole, low-fat (1% or 2%), and nonfat milk
- blindfold

What You Do

1. Have someone fill each glass with a different kind of milk and secretly record on another piece of paper which milk went into which glass. You should not know.

2. Place the three glasses next to each other. Look at and smell each one.

   Which looks the thinnest? _____ Which looks the thickest? _____

   Guess which is which: A = _____   B = _____   C = _____

   Why did you make those guesses? _____

3. Put on the blindfold. Ask the other person to give you one glass at a time in any order. Taste the milk in each glass. Guess which is which. Have the other person record your guesses:

   A = _____   B = _____   C = _____

4. Were you right in Step 2? _____ Were you right in Step 3? _____

   ☞ The way food looks is important. Whole milk looks creamier than nonfat milk. If nonfat milk looked as creamy as whole milk, do you think people would like it more?

Fat Flavor

Do you think you can tell the difference between
regular peanut butter and reduced-fat peanut butter?

What You Need
- piece of masking tape
- two identical plates
- two slices of bread
- knife
- regular peanut butter
- reduced-fat peanut butter (same brand)

What You Do

1. Put a piece of masking tape on the bottom of one plate. Then spread regular peanut butter on one slice of bread and put it on this plate. Spread reduced-fat peanut butter on the other slice of bread and put it on the other plate.

2. Shift the plates around so you lose track of which one has the tape.

3. Examine the two peanut butters by looking, smelling, and tasting each one. You can even feel it, if you don't mind getting sticky. Describe any differences in how the two:

   look _____

   smell _____

   taste _____

   feel _____

Fat Flavor

(continued)

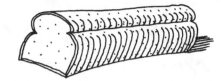

4. Guess which slice has the regular and which has the reduced-fat peanut butter. Find the tape under the plate to see if you were right.

☺ Which one did you like best?
Add your favorite jelly to it, then gobble it up as a snack.

Explain why you think it's important not to know which slice of bread is covered with which kind of peanut butter while you're doing the experiment.

_____

_____

★ *An experiment where you don't know which item you are testing is called a **blind experiment**. Using a blind experiment helps make sure that you are being fair and that the results are not affected by what you already think or know. For example, say you don't like the idea of reduced-fat peanut butter. You don't think it's as rich and creamy as the regular kind. You don't think it can possibly taste as good. That attitude would hurt your ability to judge fairly in the experiment, and that wouldn't be very scientific.*

Food Guide Pyramid Fun

List ten foods you think taste best.
Then write down the name of the food group to which each belongs.
Do your favorite foods make a balanced meal?

Your Favorite Food   **Its Food Group**

1. _____   _____

2. _____   _____

3. _____   _____

4. _____   _____

5. _____   _____

6. _____   _____

7. _____   _____

8. _____   _____

9. _____   _____

10. _____   _____

Aging Taste

In this activity you will find out if the sense of taste changes with age. Since you will need people of different ages, a family holiday gathering might be a good time to do this test.

What You Need

- can of frozen lemonade or grapefruit juice concentrate
- three bowls (labeled **1**, **2**, and **3** with masking tape)
- measuring cup
- water
- tablespoons

Person's Age	Favorite (1, 2, 3)

What You Do

1. Defrost the frozen concentrate. Label the bowls.
2. Put equal amounts of concentrate (one-third of the total) in each of the three bowls.
3. To bowl **1** (strong), add **one-sixth** the amount of water called for on the can's label. Stir.
4. To bowl **2** (regular), add **one-third** the amount of water called for. Stir.
5. To bowl **3** (weak), add **two-thirds** the amount of water called for. Stir.
6. Ask young, elderly, and middle-aged people to taste all three drinks and tell you which they like best. Record their ages and their favorites.

According to your test results, do older or younger people prefer stronger flavors?

_____

☺ Mix the drinks together to get regular juice. Gobble up!

Flavor Fun

What's your favorite flavor? Vanilla? Chocolate? Strawberry?
Most foods are a mixture of flavors. See if you like some of these.

Honey-Nut Milk

Put two tablespoons honey, two tablespoons peanut butter, and one cup cold milk into a blender. Cover and mix until the mixture is smooth. Pour it into a glass and drink it down. Does it taste more like honey or peanut butter? Try it with chocolate syrup instead of honey. Now which flavor comes through more?

Moo-Orange Juice

Fill a glass half full with cold milk. Add orange juice and stir vigorously. What happens? What does it look like? What does it taste like?

Classic Eggnog

In a covered blender at low speed, mix one egg, one tablespoon sugar, one cup cold milk, a dash of salt, and 1/4 teaspoon vanilla extract until well blended. Pour into a glass.

Before you taste the eggnog, smell the vanilla. How does it smell? Now put a dab of the vanilla on your tongue. Is it sweet, salty, bitter, or sour? Finally, taste the eggnog. Does it taste like the vanilla alone?

Wacky Water

Water is everywhere.

The water in oceans, lakes, rivers, and streams covers more than 70 percent of Earth's surface.

Water makes up about 65 percent of your weight. Except for cooking fats, all the foods you eat—even nuts and sunflower seeds—contain at least some water.

Like all other substances, water is made up of small parts called **molecules**. Molecules are made up of even smaller parts called **atoms**. Molecules of water have one atom of **oxygen** and two atoms of **hydrogen**. These atoms are held together by **bonds**.

Inside each molecule of water, the atoms are arranged so that the end of the molecule with the hydrogen atoms has a **positive** charge and the end with the oxygen atom has a **negative** charge.

Just like two magnets, the negative ends and the positive ends of different water molecules attract each other. The connections they form are called **hydrogen bonds**.

Hydrogen bonds make water behave in some wacky ways. You can explore how water behaves in the following experiments.

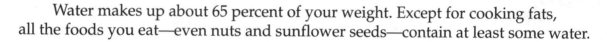

Molecular Marvels

You can't see molecules of water, but you can build models of them.

What You Need ◆ adult help

- apples
- raisins
- knife and cutting board
- wax paper
- toothpicks

What You Do

1. Cut the apple into chunks and lay the pieces on the wax paper.

2. Stick two toothpicks into each apple chunk at an angle of about 104 degrees. Stick a raisin on the other end of each toothpick. (**Hint:** Estimate this angle using your own hand. Stretch your thumb out to the side as far as possible. The angle between your thumb and pointer finger is about 90 degrees. Make the angle between the toothpicks a little more than the angle between your thumb and finger.)

☞ The apple chunks represent oxygen atoms and the raisins represent hydrogen atoms. Do you remember which end is positive and which end is negative? Arrange your molecules to show how the different ends attract each other.

☺ Gobble up your water molecules by making applesauce. Remove the toothpicks. Peel the apple chunks. Put them and the raisins into a pot. Add 1/2 cup water. Cook at medium heat until the apples are tender. Mash the apples with a spoon or fork and add honey (or sugar) and nutmeg to taste. For smoother applesauce, mix in a blender.

Food Guide Pyramid Fun

This chart shows how much water different foods contain.
In the blank space next to each food, write in the name of the food group to which it belongs.

Food	Food Group	Percent of Water
Apple (raw)		84.4
Hamburger (cooked)		54.2
Jelly bean		6.3
Tomato (raw)		93.5
Milk (whole)		87.4
Turkey		55.4
Banana (raw)		75.7
Spaghetti (cooked)		63.6
Chocolate chip cookie		3.0
Yogurt		89.0
Potato (baked)		75.1
Bread (white)		35.8
Sunflower seed kernel		4.8
Carrot (raw)		88.2

 # Water Works

You know plants need water to grow. Perhaps you've helped your mother or father
water the plants in your home or garden. Have you ever wondered
how the water gets up to the leaves from the soil?

What You Need   ◆ adult help

- celery stalks (at least two: one with leaves, one without leaves)
- at least two of the following: scallions, leeks, Swiss chard,
  leaf lettuce, asparagus, rhubarb, or other stalk vegetable or fruit
- knife and cutting board
- identical clear glasses
- water
- food coloring (red and blue)
- clock

What You Do

1. Cut the root ends off the vegetables. Trim the stalks so they are all about the same
   length. Cut the leaves off one stalk of celery.
2. Set up as many glasses as you have vegetable stalks. Add water to each of the glasses
   until they are about one-third full.
3. Add enough food coloring to each glass to color the water dark. Use a color that's
   different from the vegetable you will put in the glass.
4. Place one vegetable stalk in each glass. Look at a clock and note what time it is:

   _____

5. Check every few minutes. Note the time when the water first reaches the top of a
   vegetable stalk: _____

Water Works

(continued)

In which vegetable did the colored water reach the top first? _____

Does water travel faster in celery with leaves or without leaves? _____

Why do you think that is so? _____

6. At the end of the experiment, cut across the stalk of each vegetable.
   Where in the stalks is the color brightest? _____

   Draw a picture of how the cut surface, or cross-section, of the celery looks.

☺ You can eat the colored vegetables.
Use them in a salad or have an adult help you cook them.

★ *When you water a plant, the roots take in water from the soil. The stalk, or stem, then carries the water up to the leaves. The long, thin tubes that carry the water are called **xylem**. Water travels up a plant faster when it is needed more—for example, when the plant's leaves are dry. This is why water travels faster in the celery stalk that still has leaves. Water in the leaves **evaporates**, or dries up, making the plant feel dry.*

Fruit Jerky

Native Americans made jerky out of buffalo meat, and cowboys carried beef jerky
to eat while they were out on the trail. Jerky is strips of meat dried in the sun.
Drying the meat keeps it from spoiling. You can make fruit jerky to carry
with you when you go on a hike or play outside.

What You Need   ◆ adult help

- oven
- two or more fruits: apples, bananas, pears, peaches, plums, etc.
- knife and cutting board
- lemon juice in a small bowl
- wax paper
- kitchen scales
- cookie sheet(s)
- spatula

What You Do

1. Turn the oven on low (warm).
2. Peel, core, and cut the fruit into thin slices less than 1/4 inch thick.
3. Dip each slice into lemon juice to keep it from turning brown.
4. Put all the slices of one kind of fruit on one piece of wax paper. Weigh it on the kitchen scales. Use the chart on page 35 to record how much the fruit weighs. Repeat this step for each fruit you are using.
5. Put the fruit slices on a cookie sheet and spread them around in a single layer.
6. Place the cookie sheet in the oven. Use a spatula to turn the fruit slices over every half-hour. Leave the slices in the oven until they are completely dry (six to ten hours). When the slices are dried, remove them and let them cool.
7. Put all the slices of one kind of fruit on a piece of wax paper and weigh them. Record on the chart how much the dried fruit weighs. Do this for each fruit.

Fruit Jerky

(continued)

Fruit	Weight Before Drying	Weight After Drying

What does the dried fruit look like? _____

Does the fruit weigh more or less after drying? _____

What do you think happened? _____

Which fruit had the biggest change in weight?_____

Do you know why? Explain. _____

_____

★ *Drying food like this is called* **dehydration***. The water doesn't disappear. It evaporates, changing from a liquid into a gas (water vapor). You can store your dried fruit in a plastic bag. Be sure to remove all the air from the bag before you seal it.*

Milky Maneuvers

Sometimes the process of drying food isn't used to preserve food
as much as it is used to change one kind of food into another.

What You Need

- a plain cardboard shirt box
  (not coated or waxed)
- clean cloth handkerchief
- wire cooling rack
- 1/2 pint of heavy cream

What You Do

1. Line the box with the handkerchief and put the box on the rack.
2. Pour all the cream into the box.
3. Let the box stand undisturbed at room temperature.
4. The next day, at the same time, check to see what is happening.

   Describe the cream in the box. _____

   Taste a bit of it. What does it taste like? _____

5. Leave the box alone for another day. Check it the next day at the same time. If the
   cream is thick enough to spread but doesn't taste sour, it's ready to use. You have
   made cream cheese.

   ☺ Gobble it up on a piece of bread.

   ☹ Don't gobble it up if it tastes sour.

★ *Heavy cream is 56.6 percent water. Cream cheese is 51 percent water. By removing a little
water, you can change one food into another.*

Pop Goes the Water

Can you guess what makes popcorn pop? Here's a hint. Look at the chart on page 31. Do sunflower seeds have water inside? Do you think popcorn kernels do, too?

What You Need ◆ adult help

- popcorn kernels
- magnifying glass
- knife and cutting board
- hot-air popper or other popping method

What You Do

1. Examine several popcorn kernels with the magnifying glass. Describe what they look like. _____

2. Have an adult cut a kernel in half. Examine the inside with the magnifying glass. Do you see any water inside?_____ Describe what you see. _____

3. Pop a handful of kernels. Listen as the kernels pop. What do you think is happening?

   _____

4. Examine the popped corn. How does it differ from the kernel? Have an adult help you cut one in half. Is there any water inside? _____

★ *Corn kernels are seeds. All seeds contain a bit of water to keep them alive until they are planted and can grow. When kernels are heated quickly, the water inside turns into steam. The steam expands and pushes outward with such force that the kernels explode. The soft substance inside puffs up, and the steam disappears into the air.*

Pop or Pouf?

To prove it's the water inside the kernel that makes popcorn pop, let's try popping dried kernels and comparing them to regular ones. We'll dry our popcorn in the oven.

What You Need ◆ adult help

- oven
- popcorn kernels
- shallow baking pan
- hot-air popper or other popping method
- two bowls or containers to hold popcorn
- ruler

What You Do

1. Preheat oven to 200°F.
2. Count out 100 kernels. Spread them around the pan in a single layer. Put them in the oven for at least 90 minutes.
3. While they heat, count out another 100 fresh kernels and pop them in the popper.
4. Count the number of fresh kernels that didn't pop. Record the number on the **Results** chart on page 39.
5. Choose any ten popped kernels. Measure across the widest part of each kernel. In the **Data** chart, write down the measurements, add them together, and divide by ten. This gives you the average size to write on the **Results** chart. Record it. Think of it as a measure of "fluffiness."
6. Now go back to the dried kernels. When it is time, remove the pan from the oven. Let the kernels cool. Do they look different from fresh kernels? How?
7. Pop these dried kernels. Count the unpopped kernels and measure ten popped kernels as you did for regular popcorn kernels in Steps 4 and 5. Record your results as before. Put this popcorn in a different container.

Pop or Pouf?

(continued)

DATA		
Number	**Fresh**	**Dried**
1		
2		
3		
4		
5		
6		
7		
8		
9		
10		
Sum		
Average (÷10)		

RESULTS		
Popcorn Type	**Number Unpopped**	**Average Size**
Fresh		
Dried		

Do the fresh or the dried kernels give you fluffier popcorn? _____

Do the fresh or the dried kernels give you more popcorn? _____

☺ Keep your popcorn in separate bowls, one for fresh and one for dried. Leave both kinds plain, add salt and butter, or top with Parmesan cheese.
Then gobble up!

Which popcorn tastes better? _____

☞ Think of ways to store popcorn kernels to keep them from drying out.

Space Food

Dehydrating, or drying, foods is a good way to preserve them. It's particularly handy for foods taken into space by astronauts. Dried foods don't need refrigeration. They weigh less, and they can be packed in single servings and prepared just by adding water whenever an astronaut wants to eat.

Foods can be dehydrated by using heat from an oven the way you did in "Fruit Jerky" on pages 34–35. Foods can be dried in the sun, the process used by Native Americans and early settlers. Meat and fish can be dried using salt, which draws out the moisture. Foods can also be dried when they are frozen by using a process called *freeze-drying*.

Astronauts eat dried eggs, dried milk, and many other convenience foods that have been dehydrated. So do you. Search your kitchen cabinets for space food. Can you find any foods that are labeled freeze-dried? Can you find dry foods that are stored in foil bags or cardboard boxes and don't require refrigeration or freezing?

If you can't find any space food at home, go to the supermarket the next time your mother or father goes shopping. Read the labels on coffee jars. Look at the aisles of baking goods and prepared foods. Check out soups, rice and pasta mixes, and frozen dinners. Space food can sometimes be found in unusual places. For instance, you might even find such goodies as freeze-dried ice cream at the gift shop of your local science museum.

List all the space foods you can find.

_____   _____   _____

_____   _____   _____

_____   _____   _____

Oodles of Noodles

Some foods come dried. You have to add water before eating them.

What You Need ◆ adult help

- stove
- measuring cup
- 1/4 teaspoon salt
- large plastic container
- large bowl

- water
- large pot with lid
- eight-ounce box of egg noodles
- colander
- kitchen scale

What You Do

1. Put 12 cups of water in the pot and bring to a boil over high heat. Add salt.
2. While the water is heating, pour the noodles into the plastic container. Weigh them. Record weight here: _____
3. Add noodles to boiling water and cook as instructed on the package.
4. Place the colander in the bowl. Drain the water from the noodles into the bowl. After the water cools, use the measuring cup to see how much water there is. There are _____ cups of water, which is _____ (less/more) than before. What happened? _____
5. Pour the drained noodles into the same plastic container. Weigh them. Record weight here: _____

   Do the noodles weigh more or less after cooking? _____ Why? _____

☺ Gobble up the noodles. You can also use them to make an apple noodle pudding. In a bowl, mix two beaten eggs with six tablespoons margarine, one cup sour cream, 1/2 cup sugar, one teaspoon cinnamon, 1/2 cup raisins, and three cups sliced apples. Stir in the noodles and pour into a greased, 9 x 13-inch dish. Sprinkle nutmeg on top. Bake at 350°F. for 30 to 45 minutes.

Over the Top

Just how full is full? Do you think a full glass of water has any more room in it?

What You Need

- clear glass
- tray or shallow pan
- container of water
- powdered drink mix
- teaspoon

What You Do

1. Stand the glass on the tray.

2. Fill the glass to the brim with water so the water forms a dome but doesn't run over.

3. Slowly add one teaspoon of the powdered drink mix. Look at it from the side.

    What happens to the powder when you add it to the water?_____

    What happens to the water when you add the powder? _____

4. Add more teaspoons of powder until the water overflows. How many did you add? ___

    Why doesn't the water spill over at first? _____

    Why does it spill over eventually? _____

★ *Think of how molecules are arranged in water. The hydrogen bonds leave spaces in between molecules. At first, the powder enters those spaces and dissolves in the water. The mixture is called a* **solution**. *But once the spaces are full, no more powder can dissolve. Instead, the powder pushes the water out of the way, so the water overflows.*

Hot Stuff

Do you think temperature has an effect on how fast something dissolves?
Do you think warm water works better than cold? Let's find out.

What You Need

- three identical clear glasses (labeled **Cold**, **Room**, and **Hot** with masking tape)
- hot water, very cold water, and room temperature water
- powdered drink mix
- three teaspoons

What You Do

1. Fill each glass halfway with water at the appropriate temperature.
2. For this step, you'll need one or two helpers. At the same time, you and your helper(s) add one level teaspoon of the drink mix to each glass. As you add the powder, watch the glass from the side.

Does the powder move faster or slower in the hot water? _____

At what temperature does the powder dissolve most quickly? _____

At what temperature does the powder dissolve most slowly? _____

☞ If you wanted to make your drink very strong by dissolving a lot of powder in water, would it be best to use hot or cold water? _____ Design and carry out an experiment to test your answer.

★ *Water molecules are always moving around. Heat makes them move faster. That extra movement helps dissolve the powder.*

Speedy Solutions

Do you like races? Here's a race with solutions.

What You Need

- three or four powdered mixes: ice tea mix, lemonade mix, fruit-flavored drink mix, powdered milk, instant cream of wheat, etc.
- several identical, clear glasses
- masking tape and marker
- water at room temperature
- teaspoons

What You Do

1. Label each glass with the name of one of the powders you've selected. Then line the glasses up and fill each with the same amount of room temperature water.

2. Assign one person to each powder or mix. All at the same time, have your helpers add a teaspoon of powder to each glass. Describe what happens.

Powdered Food	What Happens to It
_____	_____
_____	_____
_____	_____
_____	_____

Which powder was the first to dissolve? _____ Does that make sense?

Did all the powders dissolve? _____ Which ones didn't? _____

☞ Now stir the ones that didn't dissolve. Does stirring help? Try putting the powders that didn't dissolve in very hot water. What happens? Why?

Salty Solutions

Why is salt put on sidewalks and streets in the winter?

What You Need

- two five-ounce paper cups
- masking tape and marker
- water at room temperature
- salt
- teaspoon
- freezer and clock
- two ice cubes

What You Do

1. Label one cup **Water** and the other cup **Salt**. Fill both cups halfway with water.

2. Add four teaspoons of salt to the cup marked **Salt**. Stir until all the salt dissolves.

3. Mark the heights of the liquids on the outside of both cups.

4. Put both cups in the freezer. Note the time: _____

5. Check the cups every half hour to see if the water has frozen.

   Which froze first? _____   Note the time: _____

   Which froze second? _____   Note the time: _____

   How much longer did it take for the second one to freeze? _____

   Now explain, if you can, why salt is put on sidewalks and streets in the winter.

☞ Put two ice cubes on the counter. Sprinkle only one with salt. Watch what happens.

☹ Don't gobble this up.

Freezing Frenzy

Make a prediction. Which will freeze first: water, juice, or a solution in between?

What You Need

- four five-ounce paper cups
- masking tape and marker
- measuring cup
- one cup clear, canned, or bottled fruit juice
- water
- four popsicle sticks
- four circles of cardboard to cover the paper cups
- freezer
- clock and/or timer

What You Do

1. Label the cups: **Juice**, **1/2**, **1/4**, and **Water**. Fill them with the amounts of juice and water shown in the chart.

Cup Label	Juice	1/2	1/4	Water
Juice	1/2 cup	1/4 cup	1/8 cup	0
Water	0	1/4 cup	3/8 cup	1/2 cup

2. Label a separate popsicle stick to match each of the four cups. Hold the matching stick in each cup so that it touches the bottom. Mark the height of the liquid on the stick.

3. Make a slit in the middle of each cardboard circle. Slide a circle over each popsicle stick. Adjust the circle and the stick so the circle rests on the cup's rim and the stick stands straight and just touches the bottom.

Freezing Frenzy

(continued)

4. Put all four cups in the freezer. Either note the time: _____ or set the timer for 30 minutes.

5. After 30 minutes, check the cups. Gently jiggle the sticks to see if the liquids have frozen. Keep checking in this way every 15 minutes until all the cups are frozen solid.

   Which liquid froze first? _____   At what time? _____

   Which liquid froze second? _____   At what time? _____

   Which liquid froze third? _____   At what time? _____

   Which liquid froze last? _____   At what time? _____

   Does water or juice freeze first? _____

   Do the liquids freeze in the same order
   as the amount of water they contain? _____

6. When all the liquids are frozen (after several hours), remove the lids and cups. Mark the level of the frozen liquid on each stick. Then . . .

☺ Gobble up your flavored popsicles. Save the sticks so you can check the markings. Which liquid expanded the most while freezing? Which juice solution behaved most like water?

★ *Read the label on the can or bottle of juice. The juice inside is a solution of fruit juice and water. The liquid in the cups marked 1/2 and 1/4 is called a **dilution**.*

Polar Pops

Look at "Food Guide Pyramid Fun" on page 31.
Do apples or bananas have more water? Which will freeze first?

What You Need ◆ adult help

- three to four fruits: melons, oranges, apples, bananas, strawberries, pears, etc.
- knife and cutting board
- popsicle sticks or toothpicks
- plastic wrap
- freezer
- clock and/or timer

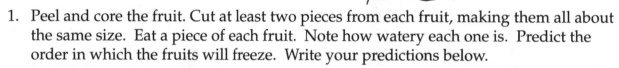

What You Do

1. Peel and core the fruit. Cut at least two pieces from each fruit, making them all about the same size. Eat a piece of each fruit. Note how watery each one is. Predict the order in which the fruits will freeze. Write your predictions below.

2. Put a popsicle stick or a toothpick into each remaining piece of fruit. Wrap each one separately with plastic wrap. Put them in the freezer. Note the time: _____

Your Prediction	**Actual Order of Freezing**
_____	_____
_____	_____
_____	_____
_____	

3. Check the fruits every half-hour to test your predictions. Write down the actual order in which the fruits froze in the chart above. Explain the results.

   ☺ Gobble up your fruit pops. Make a fruit salad with the leftover fruit.

Marvelous Mixtures

Have you ever made orange juice from a frozen concentrate, a drink from a powder, a dessert from a gelatin mix, or a salad dressing from one of those little packets?

When you mix ingredients together, you get many different results. Sometimes a powder disappears into a liquid, leaving behind only its color (if it has one). Other times, you can see particles floating around in the liquid. Still other times, two liquids won't mix.

There are many kinds of mixtures. You've already worked with solutions in earlier activities. A **solution** is a mixture in which a solid ingredient, like sugar, is dissolved in a liquid, like water. A solution has properties of both substances. Try stirring a spoonful of sugar in water. Now taste it. It's sweet, right?

Chicken noodle soup is another kind of mixture. The chicken, noodles, and vegetables never dissolve in the broth. This kind of mixture is called a **suspension**. You can see large particles in a suspension. Eventually these particles settle to the bottom. You have to stir them to get them back into suspension.

In between solutions and suspensions are mixtures called **colloids**. A colloid looks a lot like a solution, but it has particles in it like a suspension. However, its particles are much smaller—too small to see. Still, there is a way to detect them, as you'll find out!

See the Light

Look at the air around you. Do you see dust swirling around?
Now darken the room and shine a flashlight in the air. Do you see any dust?

What You Need

- four clear glasses
- masking tape and marker
- measuring cup
- water
- four teaspoons
- vinegar
- milk
- orange juice
- flashlight
- piece of cardboard with a small hole punched in the center

What You Do

1. Label the glasses **Water**, **Vinegar**, **Milk**, and **Orange Juice**.

2. P_____ of water into each glass. Add one teaspoon of water, vinegar, milk, or _____ the glass with the matching label. Stir each one with a clean spoon. _____ ids sit until the swirling stops.

_____ ht through the cardboard hole toward the glass marked **Water**. Look _____ he side. Can you see the light as it passes through the mixture?

_____ the other mixtures. In the chart on the next page, write down _____ e the light."

☹ Don't gobble up the vinegar.

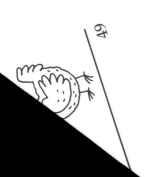

49

See the Light

(continued)

Mixture	See the Light?	Solution or Colloid?
Water	_____	_____
Vinegar	_____	_____
Milk	_____	_____
Orange Juice	_____	_____

We see things only when they give off light or *reflect* light. Reflect means to bounce back. Light bounces off things like a ball bounces off a sidewalk. In solutions, there is nothing to bounce back light, so we can't see a light beam shining through it. In contrast, colloids have particles that can reflect light so we see the beam.

Knowing this, decide which of the mixtures are solutions and which ones are colloids. Write down your answers. Then think about why you can see dust in a stream of light.

☞ Try testing other liquids in your refrigerator and kitchen cabinets. What about soda, cooking oil, maple syrup? You can even try mixtures made from powders, like instant coffee and powdered juice drinks. Can you think of other mixtures to try?

★ *More than 100 years ago, the British scientist John Tyndall discovered that colloids reflect light. This phenomenon is called **the Tyndall effect**. He also figured out why the sky is blue. (See "Blues Skies" on page 81 for the answer.)*

Gelatin Delight

Heat makes it easier to dissolve things in water. You use boiling water to make gelatin.
Do you think gelatin is a solution or a colloid?

What You Need ◆ adult help

- water
- measuring cup
- two small, clear glasses (labeled **Before** and **After** with masking tape)
- package of flavored gelatin dessert mix
- mixing bowl
- tablespoon
- stove
- flashlight and piece of cardboard with a small hole in the center

What You Do

1. Pour 1/2 cup water into each glass. Stir the gelatin mix into a bowl of boiling water as directed on the package. Stir two tablespoons of the hot mixture into the glass of water marked **Before**.

2. Add cold water to the bowl as instructed. Stir two spoonfuls of this gelatin mixture into the glass of water marked **After**. Refrigerate the rest.

3. Look at the two glasses. Do the gelatin mixtures look like solutions or colloids?
   Before: _____　　**After**: _____

4. Shine the flashlight through both glasses (see Step 3 of "See the Light" on page 50). Are the gelatin mixtures solutions or colloids?
   Before: _____　　**After**: _____

☞ Before gobbling up the gelatin from the refrigerator, look at it closely. Do you see any particles in it, or is it uniform and smooth? Hold a piece up to a light. What do you see?

Fluffy Whites

Egg white is made of protein and water. Let's see if it is a solution or a colloid.

What You Need ◆ adult help

- two eggs
  (at room temperature)
- three small glasses
- two teaspoons
- mixing bowl
- electric mixer or rotary beater

- flashlight
- piece of cardboard
  with a hole in the center
- water

What You Do

1. Separate the egg whites from the yolks (save the yolks for "Hold the Mayo," page 58).
2. Pour the whites into a glass. Shine the flashlight through the glass (see Step 3 of "See the Light" on page 50). Are egg whites a solution or a colloid? _____
3. Fill a clean glass with water. Stir in a teaspoon of egg white. Does it dissolve?_____
   Can you see particles in it? _____ Use the flashlight to be sure.
4. Pour the remaining egg whites into a bowl. Beat them until they're foamy. Pour water into another clean glass. Stir a teaspoon of the foam into the water. Does it dissolve?_____ Describe the particles you see: _____

★ *Proteins are long molecules that are wrapped around themselves. When you beat egg whites, you unravel them. This creates the foam. The long strands you see in the beaten egg white/water mixture are unraveled proteins.*

☺ Gobble up the egg whites in a meringue. Add 1/8 teaspoon salt, 1/2 teaspoon vanilla extract, and 1/2 cup sugar as you beat the egg whites into stiff peaks. Spoon the mixture onto a greased cookie sheet. Bake at 300°F. until the meringue turns light brown.

Soupy Suspension

Even though things stay separate in a suspension, the different flavors can mix together.
Taste this soup to see.

What You Need ◆ adult help

- carrots, celery, onions, other vegetables as desired
- knife and cutting board
- measuring cup and measuring spoons
- large pot with lid
- water
- seasonings: one teaspoon salt, 1/4 teaspoon pepper, 1/4 teaspoon thyme leaves
- two beef or chicken bouillon cubes
- stove
- 1/2 cup macaroni ABCs or similar small macaroni (more for a thicker soup)
- stirring spoon
- glass

What You Do

1. Select, wash, and cut up the vegetables. Put a total of two to three cups of vegetables into the pot.
2. Add eight cups water, the seasonings, and the bouillon cubes. Cover.
3. Bring to a boil over high heat. Then turn the heat to low and simmer for 30 minutes.
4. Add the macaroni. Simmer 15 minutes longer, stirring occasionally.
5. Ladle some of the soup into a glass. Let it sit on the table where you can see it while you gobble up the rest of the soup. Does anything stay suspended? _____

   What settles to the bottom first? _____   Why? _____

   Does anything float to the top? _____   Why? _____

Tasty Tartar

Not all suspensions are in liquids. Check this one out!

What You Need ◆ adult help

- pickles
- onion
- knife and cutting board
- one cup plain yogurt
- small mixing bowl
- measuring cup and measuring spoons
- spices: 1/2 teaspoon dill, 1/2 teaspoon garlic powder, dash of salt and cayenne pepper
- stirring fork

What You Do

1. Chop the pickles and onion into very small pieces.

2. Put the yogurt in the bowl. Add 1/2 cup chopped pickle and 1/3 cup chopped onion. Stir them together.

3. Add the spices. Stir until everything is mixed together.

   What ingredients can you still see? _____

   Have any ingredients disappeared? _____ Which ones? _____

   What do you think happened to them? _____

   You've just made tartar sauce. Why is it a suspension? _____

☺ Gobble up your tartar sauce the next time you have fish.
You can store it in a sealed container in the refrigerator for a few days.

All Mixed Up

Some liquids don't mix well. Stirred together, they won't make solutions.
They're said to be *immiscible*. Oil and vinegar are good examples. They won't stay mixed.
Find a clear salad dressing in the refrigerator. Can you see the separate layers
of oil and vinegar? Let's see if we can get oil and vinegar to stay together.

What You Need

- two jars with tight lids
- measuring cup and spoons
- cider vinegar, salad oil, and water
- paprika
- masking tape and marker
- clock or watch with a second hand
- one teaspoon sugar
- spices: one teaspoon salt, one teaspoon garlic powder, 1/4 teaspoon pepper

What You Do

1. Pour 1/4 cup vinegar, 1/2 cup oil, and 1/2 cup water into both jars.

2. Add one teaspoon paprika to one jar only. Label this jar **P**. Label the other jar **NP**.

3. Screw the lids on the jars. At the same time, shake each 20 times.

4. Stand the jars next to each other on the counter and note the time: _____
   Which jar has the biggest droplets of oil? _____
   In which jar does the oil separate first? _____
   Note the time when the oil in each jar separates: **NP** _____ **P** _____
   Where does the oil go? _____ Is it heavier or lighter than water? _____

All Mixed Up

(continued)

5. Shake the jar with the paprika for one minute. Put it down. Note the time: _____

   Are the oil droplets bigger or smaller than they were before? _____

   Does it take more or less time for the oil to separate? _____

   How does the size of the droplets affect how long it takes the oil to separate?

   _____

★ *Both the paprika and vigorous shaking break the oil down into tiny droplets. This makes the suspension behave like a colloid by allowing the droplets to stay mixed in the water/vinegar solution for a longer time. The smaller the oil droplets are, the longer they stay in suspension. A colloid of this sort is called an **emulsion**. Paprika and shaking are called **emulsifying agents**. They can change suspensions into colloids.*

6. To make your emulsion into French salad dressing, pour the contents of one jar into the other; then add the sugar and spices. Shake thoroughly.

☺ Gobble up on a salad.

SALAD, HO!

Hold the Mayo

When two liquids won't stay mixed, you can add a third substance to make the first two "hold" together. Such a substance is called an *emulsifying agent*.

What You Need ◆ adult help
- vinegar, oil, shallow bowl, and dish detergent
- measuring cup and measuring spoons
- blender
- two egg yolks (use the egg whites for "Fluffy Whites" on page 53)
- two tablespoons white vinegar
- two tablespoons lemon juice
- 1/4 teaspoon prepared mustard
- 1/2 teaspoon salt
- $1^1/_2$ cups salad oil

Hint: Ingredients for mayonnaise must be at room temperature.

What You Do

1. Put some vinegar into the bowl. Add a few drops of oil. Stir. Do you see droplets? Are they made of oil or vinegar? _____ Do the droplets come together or stay apart as time passes? _____

2. Add a drop of dish detergent. Stir. Soap is an emulsifying agent. What does it do to the droplets? _____ Discard the contents of the bowl.

3. To make mayonnaise, add all of the remaining ingredients (*except* the salad oil) to the blender and blend well. Pour one cup of salad oil *very* slowly into the mixture *while* it is blending. Add more oil if needed to thicken the mixture into a yellowish emulsion.

☺ Gobble up on your favorite sandwich. Store any extra mayonnaise in the refrigerator.

☞ Do you know what the emulsifying agent is in mayonnaise? How could you find out?

Food Guide Pyramid Fun

Fill in the food group to which each ingredient belongs. Then make this tasty mixture.

Ingredient	Food Group
one cup crispy rice cereal	_____
1/2 cup smooth peanut butter	_____
2 1/2 tablespoons powdered milk	_____
two tablespoons raisins	_____
two tablespoons honey (or molasses)	_____
1/4 cup coconut flakes	_____

To make peanut butter balls:

1. Pour the cereal into a small bowl.
2. Mix all the other ingredients together in another bowl.
3. Pick up a bit of the mixture and roll it into a ball using the palms of your hands.
4. Roll the balls in the cereal and put them on a plate.

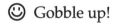

☺ Gobble up!

Butter Business

Cream, like oil in water, is a mixture of fat in water.
Shaking hard can turn the mixture inside out!

What You Need

- one-pint jar with a tight-fitting lid
- 1/2 pint heavy whipping cream
- salt
- one marble (optional)
- glass or paper cup
- rubber spatula
- cake pan
- cookie cutters

What You Do

1. Pour the cream into the jar. Sprinkle in some salt if you like salted butter.

2. Add a clean marble if you have one. Then screw on the lid.

3. Shake until the cream thickens so much you can no longer hear the marble rattling and butter has formed.

4. Drain off the liquid into the glass or cup. Taste it. It's buttermilk. Does it taste different from regular milk? _____ In what way? _____

5. Press the butter down with the spatula. Remove any liquid that comes out. Spread a thick layer of butter in the pan. Chill. Make pats of butter in fun shapes with the cookie cutters.

☺ Gobble up on bread or rolls!

☞ You turned cream inside out! Shaking made the fat droplets in the cream come together to make big globs that separated from the water. Soon, instead of fat droplets in water, there were water droplets in fat. And that's butter—a water-in-fat colloid.

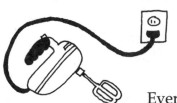

Whipped Up

Ever heard of a whipping-cream race? Here goes!

What You Need ◆ adult help
- three mixing bowls (identical if possible)
- masking tape and marker
- freezer
- one cup milk
- one cup light cream (or half-and-half)
- one cup heavy cream
- measuring cup and measuring spoons
- sugar
- vanilla extract
- three electric mixers or three rotary beaters

Doing the race with three people, each armed with a mixer, is the most fun.
If you do it alone or don't have enough mixers, you'll need a clock to time each "whipping."

What You Do

1. Label the bowls: **Milk**, **Light**, and **Heavy**. Put them in the freezer for five minutes.

2. Pour the milk, light cream, and heavy cream into the bowls using the labels as a guide.

3. Add one tablespoon sugar and one teaspoon vanilla extract to each bowl.

4. Start your engines! Beat until one turns into stiff peaks. Stop! You have a winner!

   Which one won? _____ Refrigerate it.

   Which one looks like it's going to come in second? _____

5. Continue beating the other two. Can you get both to form stiff peaks? Did the one that looked like it was going to come in second win second place? Is it easier to separate thin or thick colloids?

Maple Mix

What do you get when you mix a solution, a colloid, and a suspension?

What You Need   ◆ adult help

- maple syrup
- lemon juice (with pulp)
- melted butter
- flashlight
- piece of cardboard with a hole in the center
- measuring cup and measuring spoons
- small pan and stirring fork
- stove
- four clear glasses filled with water

What You Do

1. Just by looking at them, guess which ingredient is the solution, which is the colloid, and which is the suspension. Write your guesses in the first column below. Then use the flashlight to test your guesses (see Steps 2 and 3 of "See the Light" on page 50). Write your answers in the second column below.

    I think the syrup is the _____ . It really is a _____ .

    I think the juice is the _____ . It really is a _____ .

    I think the butter is the _____ . It really is a _____ .

2. Put 1/4 cup maple syrup, four teaspoons lemon juice, and two tablespoons butter into the pan. Stir over low heat until it's mixed well. Guess if the mixture is a solution, a colloid, or a suspension.

3. Pour a teaspoonful of the mixture into a glass of water. Check it with the flashlight. Now what do you think it is? _____

   ☺ Use your mixture to glaze, or coat, chicken while you bake or broil it. Gobble up!

Riveting Reactions

Have you ever been a chemist? Sure you have.
You're a chemist every morning when you toast a piece of bread,
wash your hands, or chew your cereal.

A **chemist** is a person who studies what makes up different things and how things change.
When you bake a cake, you are acting like a chemist. You study the list of ingredients to find
out what makes up a cake. Then you mix them and bake them. During baking, the mixture
changes from a thick liquid to a fluffy, yummy solid.

That kind of a change is called a **chemical change**. It is brought about by a **chemical reaction**.
The chemicals (the ingredients) in the mixture (the batter) react (combine) with each other to
make something new and different. There are many types of chemical reactions,
but they all start as one kind of material and end up as another.

In some types of reactions, things change color. In other types, gases are produced,
like the bubbles in soda. There are reactions that make useful items like plastics and cloth.
There are reactions that ruin things, like the reactions that cause burnt toast and rusted metal.

In the following activities, you'll get to create some of these reactions.
You will need to do "Color Changer" before you do any of the others. Have fun!

Color Changer

Chemists often work with chemicals called *acids* and *bases*. Many acids and bases are too strong to eat. Many can cause burns, but some are actually familiar foods and drinks. Chemists tell acids and bases apart with a color changer. Let's make one.

What You Need   ◆ adult help

- 1/2 small head of red cabbage (the darker the better)
- knife and cutting board
- measuring cup
- pot with lid
- water
- stove
- colander
- mixing bowl

What You Do

1. Put three cups chopped (or shredded) cabbage in the pot.
2. Add enough water to just cover the cabbage.
3. Bring to a boil; then turn heat down to low and simmer for 15 minutes.
4. Place the colander in the bowl. Drain the liquid into the bowl. Be careful. It's hot!
5. Dump the cabbage back into the pot.

    What color is the liquid? _____ Let it cool before you use it.

Acids and bases will change the liquid you just made into different colors. You will use this liquid in the following activities to show, or *indicate*, whether a substance is an acid or a base. Pour your liquid into a jar. Label the jar **Indicator**. Store it in the refrigerator.

☺ Cook thin slices of apple in butter until tender. Add to the cabbage with a dash of salt. Stir and heat through. Gobble up!

Changing Colors

Let's find out what colors the **Indicator** changes to
when it's mixed with different acids and bases.

What You Need

- vinegar
- baking soda
- dictionary
- two saucers
- paper towels (or newspaper)
- tablespoon
- Indicator (from "Color Changer" on page 64)
- eyedropper

What You Do

1. Look up vinegar and baking soda in the dictionary to find out which is an acid and which is a base.

2. Put the saucers on a paper towel. Put one tablespoon of **Indicator** in each saucer.

3. To one saucer, add vinegar drop by drop until the color changes. To the other, add baking soda pinch by pinch until the color changes.

Vinegar is a(n) _____ . It changes the **Indicator** to _____ .

Baking soda is a(n) _____ . It changes the **Indicator** to _____ .

Acids change the **Indicator** to a(n) _____ .

Bases change the **Indicator** to a(n) _____ .

☹ Don't gobble up.

Changing Colors, Too

Be a chemical detective! Use the **Indicator** to find out if foods are acids or bases.

What You Need

- assorted liquid and powdered foods
- paper towels (or newspaper)
- saucers
- tablespoon
- Indicator (from "Color Changer," page 64)
- eyedropper
- masking tape and marker

Test Substance	Acid	Base

What You Do

1. Choose liquids and powders to test.

2. On paper towels, line up as many saucers as you have substances.

3. To each, add one tablespoon **Indicator**.

4. Add one test substance to each saucer by the drop or the pinch. Rinse the dropper or your fingers in between. Label each saucer with the name of its substance. Also write the substance on the chart and check off whether it is an acid or a base. List substances that do not cause a color change here: _____ _____ _____

5. Line up the saucers in order from the strongest to the weakest acid and the weakest to the strongest base. The stronger the acid or base, the stronger the color change.

☞ Substances that do not cause a color change are not acids or bases. They are *neutral*. Test water, if you haven't already. Is it an acid, a base, or neutral?

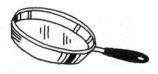

Sparkling Spinach

Have you ever been served spinach that looks limp and unappealing?
Here's a way to keep it sparkling.

What You Need   ◆ adult help

- one cup milk
- one cup water
- two small pans
- slotted spoon
- large plate
- fresh, washed spinach
- Indicator (from "Color Changer" on page 64)
- stove

What You Do

1. Put the milk in one pan and the water in the other. Heat both on low.

2. When they start to simmer, add a few leaves of spinach to each. Simmer for five minutes.

3. Use the spoon to remove the spinach from both pans to a plate. Don't empty the pans. Don't lose track of which spinach came from which pan. Compare them to a leaf of fresh spinach. Which is the brightest green? _____

   Which cooked spinach is brightest? _____

4. Taste the two cooked spinach samples. Do they taste different? _____

   Which tastes better? _____

5. Test the water from the spinach pot with the **Indicator** (see "Changing Colors," Steps 2 and 3, on page 65). Is it an acid or base? _____

6. A *buffer* is something that can remove acids and bases from solutions.

   Do you think milk or water is the buffer? _____

☺ Gobble up the uncooked spinach in a salad.

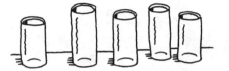

Fizzing Fun

Let's see what happens when you mix a base with an acid.

What You Need

- Indicator (from "Color Changer" on page 64)
- selection of drinks
- vinegar
- baking soda
- measuring cup and measuring spoons
- tall glasses

What You Do

1. If you haven't already done "Changing Colors" on page 65, do it now. Write down the results here, too.

   Vinegar changes the **Indicator** to _____ . It is a(n) _____ .

   Baking soda changes the **Indicator** to _____ . It is a(n) _____ .

2. Pour 1/2 cup vinegar into a tall glass. Add 1/2 teaspoon baking soda.

   Is there a reaction? _____ What does it produce? _____

3. Line up the rest of the glasses. Pour 1/2 cup of a different drink into each one.

4. To each glass add 1/2 teaspoon baking soda.

5. Which drinks have reactions? Which ones don't? Record your results on the chart on page 69. Based on the experiment with vinegar, write down whether you think each drink is an acid or a base.

Fizzing Fun
(continued)

Drinks That React		Drinks That Don't React	
Drink	Acid or Base?	Drink	Acid or Base?

6. Which drink do you think is the strongest acid? _____

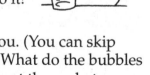

☞ What could you use to find out if your conclusions are right? Do it!

☺ Taste your fizzing drinks. At least take a sip. They won't hurt you. (You can skip the drink you made with vinegar.) Do you like how they taste? What do the bubbles feel like on your tongue? Did you end up with something different than what you started with?

★ *When baking soda reacts with acids, it gives off a gas called **carbon dioxide**, the same gas that forms bubbles in soda, the same gas that you breathe out. Carbon dioxide comes from the breakdown of the baking soda, which contains carbon and oxygen as well as sodium and hydrogen.*

Fizzing Power

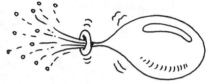

Can you blow up a balloon without blowing into it? Sure you can!

What You Need

- box of baking soda
- Indicator (from "Color Changer" on page 64)
- can of double-acting baking powder
- two identical, large, round balloons
- measuring cup and tablespoon

- vinegar
- funnel

What You Do

1. Read the labels on the baking soda box and the baking powder can. Do they have an ingredient in common? What is it? _____

2. Test vinegar, baking soda, and baking powder with the **Indicator** (see page 65).

   Vinegar changes the **Indicator** to _____ . It is a(n) _____ .

   Baking soda changes the **Indicator** to _____ . It is a(n) _____ .

   Baking powder changes the **Indicator** to _____ . It is a(n) _____ .

3. Insert the funnel into the neck of one balloon. Pour one tablespoon of baking powder into the funnel. Shake to get all the powder into the balloon.

4. Hold the balloon and funnel over a sink. Quickly pour in 1/4 cup vinegar, remove the funnel, and pinch the neck of the balloon shut. What happens? Now open your fingers a bit.

   Was there a reaction? _____ What did it produce? _____

5. Repeat Steps 3 and 4 using the other balloon and one tablespoon baking soda instead of baking powder. Which causes a bigger reaction? _____

   ☞ Can you get the balloon really big? Try different amounts of the ingredients.

Food Guide Pyramid Fun

Read these lists of ingredients. Guess what food each list of ingredients makes.
The main ingredient is listed first. Write the food group next to each main ingredient.
Are any of the ingredients acids? Are any bases? Check them out!

Ingredients 1 = _____

tomatoes _____
water
corn syrup
wheat flour
salt
vegetable oil
spices
ascorbic acid
citric acid

Ingredients 2 = _____

corn syrup _____
sugar
water
cocoa
a preservative
oil derivatives
xanthum gum
an emulsifier
vanilla flavoring

Ingredients 3 = _____

soybeans _____
water
wheat
salt
vinegar
a preservative

Ingredients 4 = _____

wheat flour _____
cracked wheat
vegetable oil
salt
baking soda
whey
barley flour
yeast

[Answers: 1 = tomato soup; 2 = chocolate syrup; 3 = soy sauce; 4 = wheat crackers]

Flat or Fluffy?

In a cookbook, find ten recipes for cakes. How many of them use baking soda and/or baking powder? Do you know why?

What You Need   ◆ adult help

- oven
- muffin tin with four cups lined with paper baking cups
- masking tape and marker
- large mixing bowl
- measuring cup and measuring spoons
- one cup sifted flour
- 2/3 cup sugar
- 1/2 bar softened butter
- 2/3 cup milk
- one egg
- 1/4 teaspoon salt
- one teaspoon vanilla extract
- electric mixer and four mixing bowls (labeled **1**, **2**, **3**, and **4**)
- baking soda and double-acting baking powder
- large spoon (or ladle)

What You Do

1. Preheat oven to 350°F. Label the cups in the muffin tin **1**, **2**, **3**, and **4**.

2. Into the large bowl, measure out all the ingredients except the baking soda and baking powder. Beat at low speed until well mixed. Then beat at medium speed for three minutes. Divide the batter equally among the four labeled bowls.

3. To bowl **1**, add one teaspoon baking soda. To bowl **2**, add one teaspoon baking powder. To bowl **3**, add one teaspoon of each. Don't add anything to bowl **4**.

Flat or Fluffy?

(continued)

4. Beat each batter at medium speed for two more minutes. Spoon batter from each bowl into the muffin cup with the matching number; fill each cup halfway.

5. Bake for 15 to 20 minutes until golden brown. Allow to cool.

6. Compare the four cupcakes. Are they all the same height? Which is the flattest? Which is the fluffiest? Cut the cupcakes in half. Do they look different inside? Do they taste different? Use the space below to describe the four cupcakes. Circle the one you like best.

    Cupcake **1** _____

    Cupcake **2** _____

    Cupcake **3** _____

    Cupcake **4** _____

    If you wanted to make perfect cupcakes, would you have to add baking soda? _____

    Would you have to add baking powder? _____

7. Read the labels on the baking soda box and the baking powder can. Does one of them contain an acid? _____ Does knowing that help explain your results? _____

    What made your cupcakes bake differently? _____

    _____

☞ Many breads use something else to rise. Find out what it is.

★ *Double-acting baking powder contains one base and two acids. One acid reacts with the base (and releases gas) in the batter. The other needs heat to react. To see this at work, spoon baking powder into cool water, wait a minute, then add hot water.*

Frazzled Fruit

Have you ever seen a piece of fruit turn brown? That's a reaction.

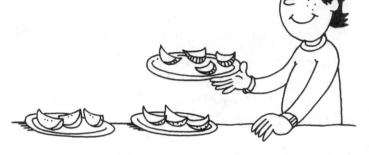

What You Need ◆ adult help

- apple, pear, peach, or banana
- knife and cutting board
- two small plates
- plastic wrap
- refrigerator
- clock

What You Do

1. Start with a piece of fruit at room temperature. Peel and cut it into four pieces.
2. Put a piece on each plate. Wrap the other two pieces separately in plastic wrap.
3. Put one plate with fruit and one wrapped fruit in the refrigerator. Leave the others out.
4. At first, check all four every 15 minutes. After 30 minutes, check them every half hour. Write down the order in which the pieces of fruit turned brown.

1st _____   2nd _____

3rd _____   4th _____

Plastic wrap keeps things from being exposed to the air. What could that have to do with the fruit turning brown? _____
Does the cold temperature of the refrigerator make the reaction happen faster or slower? _____

☺ Gobble up the fruit. Does brown fruit taste different or just look different?

★ *The browning of fruit is a reaction called* **oxidation**. *Oxygen in the air reacts with a substance in the fruit. Rusting metal is another example of oxidation.*

Keep It Fresh

Good cooks know a secret way to keep fruit from turning brown.

What You Need   ◆ adult help

- five small bowls and five small plates
- apple, pear, peach, or banana
- orange or lemon juice
- vitamin C tablet (optional)
- knife and cutting board
- water
- milk
- clock

What You Do

1. Leave one bowl empty. Fill one bowl with water, one with milk, and one with orange juice or lemon juice. If you have a vitamin C tablet, dissolve it in one cup of water and pour the solution into a fifth bowl. Line up the plates in front of the bowls.

2. Peel and slice the fruit. Put several slices in each bowl. If the bowl contains a liquid, make sure the liquid covers the fruit.

3. After a few minutes, move the slices from the first bowl to its plate. Rinse your fingers. Repeat by moving the fruit from each bowl to its plate and rinsing your fingers in between.

4. Examine the fruit on the plates every half hour for as many hours as you want.

   Did the fruit that was soaked in water turn brown more slowly than the fruit that was not soaked at all? _____ What about the fruit soaked in milk? _____

   Which liquids cause fruit to take a long time to turn brown? _____

   Can you guess what's in those liquids that prevents browning? _____

   ☺ Gobble up a fresh fruit salad preserved in the way you think works best.

Bean Sprouts

People need both acids and bases in their diet. What about plants? What do they need?

What You Need

- five plastic cups (labeled **Water**, **Milk**, **Cola**, **Orange Juice**, and **Baking Soda**)
- tray or shallow pan
- solution of one teaspoon baking soda in one cup water
- liquids: water, milk, cola, orange juice
- potting soil
- 15 bean seeds
- ruler

What You Do

1. Put soil in each cup. Plant three seeds in each, covering them lightly with soil. Place the cups on a tray in a sunny spot.

2. Every day, add to each cup three tablespoons of the liquid that matches the label on the cup.

3. Measure the height of the plants after one week and after two weeks.

    After one week, _____ is the tallest and _____ is the shortest.

    After two weeks, _____ is the tallest and _____ is the shortest.

    Do any of the plants look sickly? Which ones? _____

4. You've probably already tested these liquids with the **Indicator**. If you haven't, do it now (see Steps 2 and 3 of "Changing Colors" on page 65).

    Which liquids are bases? _____ acids? _____

    Which are neutral or buffers? _____

5. Fill in the blanks after observing the bean plants: Plants grow best in _____ (write in the name of one of the liquids). Acids are _____ (good, not good) for plants. Bases are _____ (good, not good) for plants. _____ (write in one of the liquids) acts most like water for feeding plants.

Colorful Creations

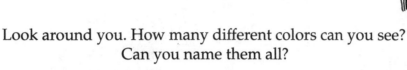

Look around you. How many different colors can you see?
Can you name them all?

Now imagine a world without color. What would it look like?
A rose wouldn't be red. An orange wouldn't be orange. The grass wouldn't be green,
and the sky wouldn't be blue.

Color has always existed. But people who lived long ago didn't know where color came from.
Then a scientist in England, named Isaac Newton, discovered something special about
sunlight. He found that he could make it turn into a rainbow of colors.

That was nearly 300 years ago. Since then, we've learned a lot more about color
and how we see it. Our eyes can see something only when it gives off light (like a flame)
or reflects light. Reflect means to bounce back. Objects reflect light like a sidewalk
reflects a ball. If they didn't, they'd be invisible.

The light from the sun and electric bulbs contains the colors of the rainbow.
However, most things cannot reflect all those colors. If they did, they would look white.
Instead, inside objects there are chemicals, called pigments, that absorb some of the colors
in light and reflect others. The colors these pigments reflect determine the colors we see.
The pigments in a red apple reflect red light, so the apple looks red.
Those in a banana reflect yellow light, so the banana looks yellow.

 # Rainbow Bright

Pretend you are Isaac Newton. Ask yourself, what color is the light from the sun?

What You Need

- prism (or a wine glass filled with water)
- one piece of white paper
- crayons or colored markers

What You Do

1. In a darkened room, hold the prism so sunlight from a window shines through it and onto the paper. (**Hint:** To sharpen the source of light, hold a piece of cardboard with a slit cut in the center between the light and the prism.) What colors do you see? Write them down in the order you see them, from left to right.

   _____   _____   _____   _____   _____   _____

2. On page 80, in the box labeled **Sunlight**, color the rainbow that you see on the paper. Draw the colors in the order you see them.

★ *When light travels from air into glass or from air into water, its speed changes. That causes it to change direction or bend. This is called **refraction**. Different colors travel at different speeds and therefore are bent to different degrees. This determines their order in a rainbow. Red light is the slowest and therefore bends the least. Raindrops, like prisms, split light into its colors. Because light is being bent, rainbows are curved.*

☞ To see the effect of bending light, put a straw in a glass of water. Look at it from the side. Is something odd? Did something happen to the straw?

 # Rainbow Light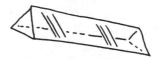

Is light from a flashlight or light bulb the same as sunlight? Can it make a rainbow?

What You Need

- flashlight and lamp
- prism (or a wine glass filled with water)
- one piece of white paper
- crayons or colored markers

What You Do

1. In a darkened room, shine the flashlight through the prism onto the white paper.
   (**Hint:** To sharpen the source of light, hold a piece of cardboard with a slit cut in the
   center between the light and the prism.) What colors do you see? Write them down in
   the order you see them, from left to right.

   _____ _____ _____ _____ _____ _____

   On page 80, in the box labeled **Flashlight**, color the rainbow that you see.

2. Repeat Step 1 with light from a household lamp. What colors do you see? In what
   order?

   _____ _____ _____ _____ _____

3. On page 80, in the box labeled **Lamp**, color the rainbow that you see. Compare these
   drawings to the one you made for **Sunlight**. Are the same colors in all three drawings?
   _____ Are the colors in all three in the same order? _____

★ *The colors in white light are always refracted in the same order, but you may not see all the
colors. Sunlight is separated evenly into all colors of the spectrum, but incandescent light has
more red than blue in it, so its rainbow may look different.*

 # Rainbow Drawings

Use this page to draw your rainbows from "Rainbow Bright" and "Rainbow Light."

Sunlight

Flashlight

Lamp

Blue Skies

Light travels in a straight line, but you can make it bounce and look blue!

What You Need

- piece of cardboard with a shiny white surface, or cardboard covered with aluminum foil
- flashlight
- small fishbowl or round glass
- water
- milk

What You Do

1. Hold the cardboard so the shiny side faces a white wall. Shine the flashlight on the shiny surface. Where does the light go? Does all of it stay on the cardboard or does some of it appear on the wall? _____

2. Fill the fishbowl with water. Stir in a few drops of milk.

3. In a darkened room, shine the flashlight through the bowl from a few feet away.

4. Look at the bowl from different directions.

   Can you see a bluish color? _____ From which direction? _____

   What other colors can you see? _____

☞ Try adding more or less milk. Try moving the light back and forth. What works best?

☺ Use blue food coloring to make a glass of blue milk. Gobble up.

★ *Remember the Tyndall effect described on page 51 of "See the Light"? In water, milk makes a colloid. The milk particles reflect light in all directions, but they scatter blue light more than other colors. In this way, they behave like the gases in the air above Earth, which is why our sky is blue. On the moon, the sky is black. On Venus, it is red!*

Food Guide Pyramid Fun

Figure out the clues on this page and write the answers below. Then complete the crossword puzzle on the next page by filling in the name of each food. Snack on a colorful fruit kabob. Cut up apples, kiwi, oranges, and other favorites, put them on skewers, and then gobble up!

	Food	**Color**
Across		
1. The name of this small, round fruit begins with the color of the sky	_____	_____
3. Eating one of these fruits a day is said to keep the doctor away	_____	_____
5. Drink this to make your bones strong	_____	_____
6. A long, thin vegetable that is good for your vision	_____	_____
Down		
1. These vegetables can be stringy, or Italian, or wax.	_____	_____
2. A purple vegetable that's not egg-y at all	_____	_____
4. This sour fruit makes a great summertime drink	_____	_____

Food Guide Pyramid Fun

(continued)

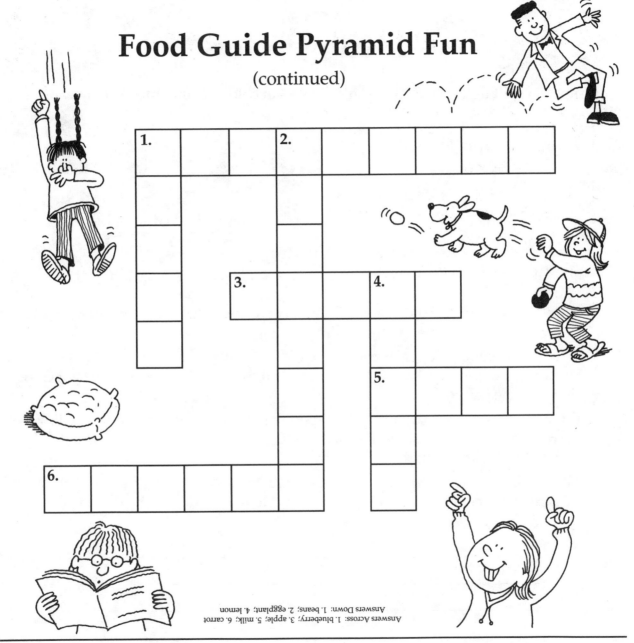

Mixing Colors

You can split light into colors. You can also put colors together to make new ones.

What You Need

- three small bowls
- water
- measuring cup
- red, blue, and yellow food coloring
- three teaspoons
- three small, clear glasses

What You Do

1. Add 1/3 cup of water to each bowl. Add three drops of red food coloring to one bowl, three drops of blue food coloring to the second, and three drops of yellow to the third. Use a clean spoon for each one and stir.

2. Mix one teaspoon red water and one teaspoon blue water in a glass. What color did the water in the glass turn? _____ Fill in the color wheel on the next page. Rinse and dry the teaspoons.

3. Now, in a separate glass, mix one teaspoon of red with one teaspoon of yellow. Be sure to rinse and dry the spoons after each use. In the same way, mix yellow with blue. Fill in the color wheel with the colors you get.

4. Try mixing colors in other amounts. Can you make dark green? pale orange? black? Use the lines below to keep track of which colors you add and how much of each you use.

_____

_____

_____

Mixing Colors
(continued)

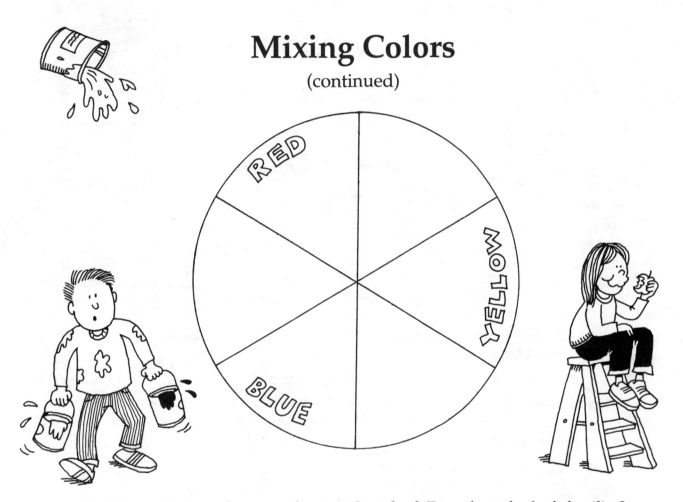

Read the colors in order around your color wheel. Does the order look familiar?

☞ At a local paint store, gather lots of different color samples. Cut them into single squares of colors, then line them up to make an elaborate rainbow.

☺ Gobble up a food in your favorite color.

Rainbow Creation

Make a rainbow you can eat!

What You Need ◆ adult help

- stove, refrigerator
- one small box each of red, blue, and yellow gelatin dessert mix
- three mixing bowls
- measuring cup
- water
- three spoons
- large, sealable, plastic bag
- masking tape

What You Do

1. Follow directions on the boxes to make the gelatin mixes in separate bowls to the point where the gelatin is ready to chill.

2. While chilling the mixtures for 45–50 minutes, stir each a few times with a clean spoon.

3. When the gelatin is partially set, spoon each color into the plastic bag to make three separate stripes, with yellow in the middle. Smooth all the air out of the bag, then seal it. Tape over the seal.

4. Squish neighboring colors of gelatin together.

   What new colors appear? _____

   Where do they appear? _____

   Which color of the rainbow is missing? _____ Why?

   ☺ Gobble up! Squeeze the gelatin out of the bag and into a bowl.
   Do the new colors have new flavors?

Night Gel

Bored with the usual gelatin colors? Try this.

What You Need

- stove, refrigerator
- one small box each of red, blue, and yellow gelatin dessert mixes
- three mixing bowls
- measuring cup
- water
- spoons

What You Do

1. Following the directions on the boxes, make the gelatin mixes in separate bowls to the point where you add cold water.

2. Try to make black gelatin by testing different combinations of the colored gelatin. Look back at your results from "Mixing Colors" on page 84. Note what colors you use. (**Hint:** To make black, you might have to first make the three other colors of the rainbow.)

3. If the gelatin starts to gel, warm it up.

4. Once you're satisfied you have black gelatin, measure how much you have. Put it in a bowl and add an equal amount of cold water. Refrigerate.

Write down all the colors you put into your black gelatin.

_____

☺ Gobble up! What does it taste like?

Splitting Colors

You've put colors together. Now pull them apart.

What You Need

- tall glasses
- one-inch strips of paper towels longer than the glasses are tall
- different-colored, felt-tipped markers (not waterproof)
- water
- clothes hanger (optional)

What You Do

1. On one strip of paper towel, about two inches from one end, draw a thick line across the width of the strip with one of the markers. Label the other end of the strip with the name of the color. Repeat with the other strips, using a different color marker for each.
2. Fill each glass with one inch of water. Place two to three paper strips in each glass so the ends that are labeled drape one inch over the rim and the other ends are in the water. The lines of color must be above the water.
3. While you are waiting, make predictions about what colors from each marker will show on the paper towel. Circle the color you think will split into the other colors best.

Marker Color	I Predict These Colors Will Appear
_____	_____
_____	_____
_____	_____
_____	_____
_____	_____

Splitting Colors
(continued)

4. When the strips are completely wet, record what colors actually came out of each marker. Hang the strips over the hanger to dry.

Marker Color	Colors That Appeared
_____	_____
_____	_____
_____	_____
_____	_____
_____	_____

How good were your predictions? Did you base them on results from other activities, or were they just guesses? What color split best? Did you guess that color?

Can you explain what happened? Think about solutions (dissolving substances in water) as well as color mixtures.

★ *Molecules of different-colored dyes stick to the paper to different degrees, so they are removed at different rates by the water traveling through the colored stripe. As the molecules are removed, they dissolve in the water and travel with it. This process is called* **paper chromatography**. *It comes from the Greek word* **khroma**, *meaning color.*

Splitting Juices

How many foods can you find that are more colorful that they look?

What You Need ◆ adult help

- tall glasses
- one-inch strips of paper towels longer than the glasses are tall
- water
- fruit juices
- assorted vegetables and fruits
- blender or juicer
- straws

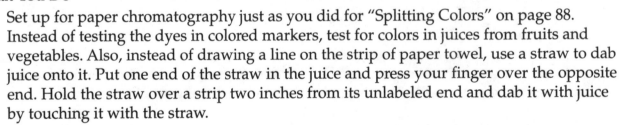

What You Do

Set up for paper chromatography just as you did for "Splitting Colors" on page 88. Instead of testing the dyes in colored markers, test for colors in juices from fruits and vegetables. Also, instead of drawing a line on the strip of paper towel, use a straw to dab juice onto it. Put one end of the straw in the juice and press your finger over the opposite end. Hold the straw over a strip two inches from its unlabeled end and dab it with juice by touching it with the straw.

1. Test fruit juices and juices you make by processing colorful foods like carrots, beets, and raspberries in a blender or juicer. Remember to clean the blender between each use. You can even test mixtures of two or more juices by stirring them together before you dab the paper strip.

2. Keep track of what you test and record your results in the chart on the next page. Write down the juice you are testing, its original color, and what colors, if any, appear.

☞ Don't gobble up all the juices. Save some of them (in covered containers in the refrigerator) for "Milk Magic" on page 92.

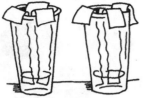

Splitting Juices
(continued)

Juice	Original Color	Colors That Appear
_____	_____	_____
_____	_____	_____
_____	_____	_____
_____	_____	_____
_____	_____	_____
_____	_____	_____
_____	_____	_____
_____	_____	_____

Are you surprised by any of your results? _____

What did you expect would happen that didn't? _____

_____

What did happen that you didn't expect? _____

_____

★ *Sometimes results are surprising. Colored juices you expect to separate won't always do that.*
Their pigments may not be soluble in water.

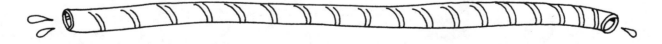

Milk Magic

Do you like to paint? Here's a paint you can eat!

What You Need

- instant dry milk powder
- small bowls
- spoons
- water
- colored juices (from "Splitting Juices" on page 90)
- plain sugar cookies

Hint: It's okay to substitute regular milk. You'll just get a thinner paint.

What You Do

1. Put two to three spoonfuls of dry milk powder into each bowl.

2. For the first bowl, count the spoonfuls of water you add as you stir one spoonful at a time into the powder to make a thick liquid. Add the same number of spoonfuls of water to the other bowls and stir.

3. To each bowl, add one of the colored juices you made in "Splitting Juices" on page 90 (or make them now). Add enough juice to get the color you want, but don't make the liquid too thin. Mix up some new colors if you want (see "Mixing Colors" on page 84).

4. Use your finger to paint plain sugar cookies. Let them dry.

☺ Gobble up!

☞ "Paint" bread and then toast it for a special effect. Or paint one another's faces!

Delectable Dips

What You Need ◆ adult help

- blender
- 1/2 cup softened cream cheese
- one cup plain (or vanilla) yogurt
- two teaspoons lemon juice
- one package each of defrosted frozen raspberries, blueberries, and strawberries
- six bowls
- three spoons
- your choice of apples, pears, and melons for dipping
- knife and cutting board

What You Do

1. Blend the cream cheese, yogurt, and lemon juice together until the mixture is smooth.

2. Divide the mixture among three bowls. Clean the blender.

3. Puree the raspberries, blueberries, and strawberries separately and pour into three other bowls. Remember to clean the blender each time.

4. Stir different amounts of the fruit purees into the bowls of cream cheese mixture to create your own colorful dips.

5. Cut apples, pears, and melons into large pieces.

☺ Dip the fruit in the dips and gobble up!

What color do you get from . . .

raspberries? _____ blueberries? _____ strawberries? _____

☞ What other fruits could you use to make dips? What colors would they give you?

Egg-citing Dyes

Add some color to your breakfast, lunch, or snack!

What You Need   ◆ adult help

- stove
- water
- measuring cup and measuring spoons
- small pan
- three or four Spanish onions
- colander
- bowl
- vinegar
- three or four yellow onions
- other vegetables and fruits
- coffee cups
- unpeeled, hard-boiled eggs

What You Do

1. Boil the dry outer skins from several Spanish onions in two cups of water for five minutes. Strain the liquid into a bowl. Add one tablespoon vinegar to the liquid and stir.

   What color is the dye? _____

2. Repeat Step 1 with yellow onions for a peach color. Other vegetables, like red cabbage, will give you dyes when boiled or soaked in boiling water. Try several.

3. Also try juices from vegetables and fruits (see "Splitting Juices" on page 90).

Egg-citing Dyes
(continued)

4. Write the food you use and the color it makes below.

Food	**Dye Color**
_____	_____
_____	_____
_____	_____
_____	_____
_____	_____
_____	_____

5. Let the dyes cool, then pour them into cups. Add one teaspoon vinegar for each 1/2 cup dye.

6. Put one egg in each cup of dye. Do all of the dyes work? _____

    Which dyes don't work? _____

☺ Peel and gobble up your colorful eggs!

Green Spaghetti

For a change in scenery, make some green spaghetti.

What You Need   ◆ adult help

- box of spaghetti
- large pot with lid
- water
- fresh basil
- measuring cup
- 1/3 cup olive oil
- 1/4 cup grated Parmesan cheese
- 1/2 teaspoon salt
- 1/8 teaspoon garlic powder
- blender
- stove

What You Do

1. Cook the spaghetti as instructed on the box.

2. Remove enough leaves from the basil to fill three cups. Discard the stems.

3. Put three cups of basil leaves, the oil, cheese, salt, and garlic into the blender.

4. Cover and blend at medium speed until it forms a thick paste.

5. Pour the sauce over a plate of hot spaghetti. Stir and serve.

☺ Gobble up!

Which ingredient makes the sauce green? _____

☞ This ingredient is a plant. At the library,
find out what's inside plants that makes them green.

Dynamic Digestion

Food wouldn't do you any good if you didn't have a way to digest it, take nutrients out of it, and get rid of the waste. Those jobs are done by your digestive system.

The **digestive system** starts in your mouth, where your teeth begin the process by chewing food. Certain foods are broken down even more in a chemical reaction with saliva. Your tongue gets into the act by moving food around and by helping you swallow.

Now your food enters a long tube called the **esophagus**. Like a hand squeezing a tube of toothpaste, muscles that line the esophagus contract and squeeze the food down into the stomach. In your stomach, which has lots of muscles, the food is twisted and churned like clothes in a washing machine. Chemicals in the stomach fluid react with the food and break it down even more.

After two to five hours in the stomach, the food travels into an incredibly long, narrow, curving tube. This tube, called the **small intestine**, is more than 20 feet long! All along its length, more chemicals, some from the liver, keep digesting the food.

Soon the food is so broken down that the **nutrients**—the parts of food that help you grow—are separated from the rest of the food. These nutrients, including proteins, vitamins, and sugars, pass through the wall of the small intestine into your bloodstream. Your heart pumps the blood around your body, delivering the nutrients everywhere.

The parts of the food that you can't use are sent to the **large intestine**, which eliminates these leftovers from your body.

Pizza People

Where does food go after you swallow it? How do nutrients get around your body?

What You Need ◆ adult help

- prepared pizza dough
- pizza toppings: sauce, cheese, sausage, pepperoni, onions, etc.
- large gingerbread man cookie cutter
- baking pan
- oven

What You Do

1. Preheat oven as directed for the pizza dough.

2. Use the cookie cutter to cut people shapes out of the dough (or shape them by hand). Place them on the pan.

3. Use various toppings to "draw" in the parts of the digestive system on some of the pizza people and the circulatory system on others. For example, use sausage for the stomach, pepperoni for the liver, pieces of shredded cheese for the esophagus, and sliced strips of onion for the intestines. (See page 99 for diagram.)

4. Bake as directed.

☺ As you gobble up your pizza, call out the part of the body you're eating.

Pizza People
(continued)

DIGESTIVE SYSTEM

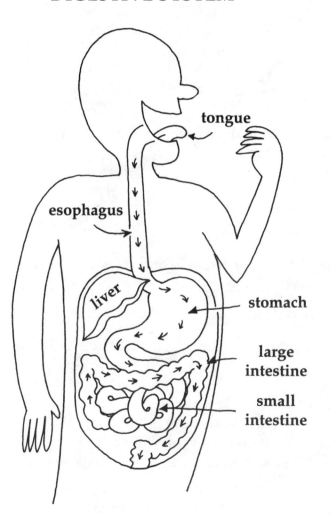

CIRCULATORY SYSTEM

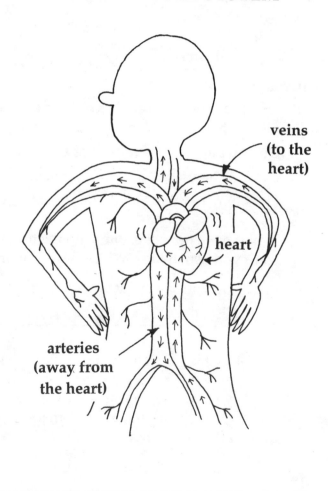

Choppers or Chewers?

Look into a mirror. Open wide and look at your "pearly whites." That's a nickname for teeth. Do your front teeth look different from your back teeth? Do you know why?

What You Need

- piece of lettuce
- apple
- slice of bologna

What You Do

1. One at a time, bite off pieces of the lettuce, the apple, and the bologna. Chew each piece. Then swallow it. Pay attention to which teeth you use.

   Do you bite with your front or back teeth? _____

   Do you chew with your front or back teeth? _____

   Does it matter what food you are eating? _____

2. Now do the opposite. Bite with the teeth you usually use to chew, and chew with the teeth you usually use to bite. Does it work as well? _____

   What can you say about why your front and back teeth are shaped the way they are?

   _____

   ☺ Gobble up a bologna and lettuce sandwich with an apple for dessert.

   ☞ While you gobble up your sandwich, think about this. People eat both plants and meat, so we have teeth to do both jobs. Deer only eat grasses. What kind of teeth do you think they have? Wolves only eat meat. What kind of teeth do you think they have?

Teeth Treats

When sailors were away at sea, they used to carve designs into whales' teeth.
The beautiful decorations were called *scrimshaw*.

What You Need

- white icing
- ice cream cone (cone-shaped)
- knife
- blue food coloring
- toothpicks
- small bowl
- mirror

What You Do

1. Spread icing around the *outside* of the cone.

2. In a small bowl, color a bit of leftover icing with the blue food coloring. Dip a toothpick in the colored icing and use it to draw scrimshaw designs on your cone "tooth."

3. Look at your own teeth in a mirror. Point to the teeth that look most like the cone tooth. Those teeth are called canines.

   How many canine teeth do you have? _____

   What kinds of food do you think canines are used to bite or chew? _____
   Test your answer the next time you eat a meal.

☺ Gobble up your cone tooth for dessert! Be sure to brush your teeth after sugary snacks.

Soaking Shells

The snack you made in "Teeth Treats" is not good for your teeth. Do you know why?

What You Need

- three cups (labeled **Water**, **Vinegar**, and **Sugar)**
- one teaspoon sugar
- water
- vinegar
- eggshells (from one egg)

What You Do

1. In the cup labeled **Sugar,** stir the sugar into 1/4 cup water to make a sugar solution. Pour 1/4 cup water into the cup labeled **Water** and 1/4 cup vinegar into the cup labeled **Vinegar**.
2. Put pieces of eggshells into all three cups. The shells should be covered by the liquid.
3. Let the shells soak at least one full day. Look at the cups. Are there shells left in each cup?
4. Examine the shells that are left by looking at and touching them. Describe the shells.

Water _____

Vinegar _____

Sugar _____

Is sugar as bad for teeth as vinegar? _____

☞ Vinegar is an acid. What can you say about acids and teeth?

★ *Bacteria in your mouth eat sugar and give off acid as a waste product.*
Teeth, like eggshells, are mostly made of calcium. Acid decomposes teeth, causing cavities.

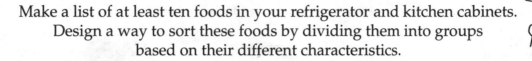

Food Guide Pyramid Fun

Make a list of at least ten foods in your refrigerator and kitchen cabinets.
Design a way to sort these foods by dividing them into groups
based on their different characteristics.

For example, first you could group the foods according to whether they are eaten by
plant-eaters (*herbivores*) or meat-eaters (*carnivores*). Then you could divide the foods
in those groups by whether or not you like them and then by the food group
they belong to. You can also group foods by their color, texture, or shape.

See how many different ways you can sort the same foods. Draw your different plans
on another piece of paper. List the foods that belong in each group.

Here's an example of a simple plan.

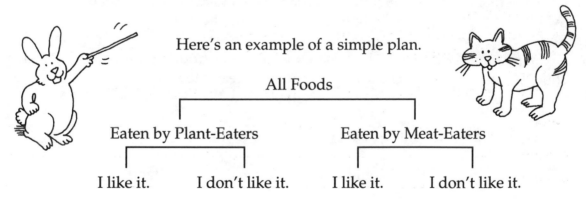

All Foods

Eaten by Plant-Eaters   Eaten by Meat-Eaters

I like it.   I don't like it.   I like it.   I don't like it.

★ *Scientists use classification systems like your plans to help understand the similarities and
differences among things. The most important classification system is the one that groups
living things into animals, plants, and other categories for simpler organisms.*

Melt in Your Mouth

Did you know that your mouth is like a chemistry laboratory?

What You Need

- miniature marshmallows
- chocolate chips
- nuts
- clock with a second hand

What You Do

1. Place one miniature marshmallow on your tongue. Let it sit there. Watch the clock. Does the marshmallow "melt"? How long does it take for it to be ready to swallow? Swallow and record your findings on the chart on the next page.
2. Repeat Step 1 with the chocolate and the nuts. Record the times on the chart.
3. Do Steps 1 and 2 again, but this time move the food around with your tongue. Don't chew! Time how long it takes for the food to be ready to swallow. Record your results.
4. Repeat the process once more, but this time, chew the food. Record your results.

Which food do you think would be the easiest to digest? _____

Which food do you think would require the most work to digest? _____

★ *During digestion, both physical and chemical changes occur in food. Chewing chops food into smaller pieces. That's a physical change. Saliva contains a chemical called an **enzyme** that reacts with and breaks down starch in foods. This is a chemical change.*

Melt in Your Mouth

(continued)

Action	Food	Did It Melt?	How long?
Sit on Tongue	Marshmallow		
	Chocolate chip		
	Nut		
Move with Tongue	Marshmallow		
	Chocolate chip		
	Nut		
Chew	Marshmallow		
	Chocolate chip		
	Nut		

☺ Sprinkle a few marshmallows, chips, and nuts into a bowl of yogurt. Gobble up!

Enzyme Action

Your stomach's a chemistry lab, too. Here's how one stomach chemical works.

What You Need ◆ adult help
- four bowls (labeled **None, Cold, Lukewarm,** and **Hot)**
- package of junket (or substitute rennet, available at health food stores)
- measuring cup and measuring spoons
- milk
- saucepan
- stove
- refrigerator

What You Do

1. Put $1^1/2$ tablespoons of junket in the three bowls labeled **Cold, Lukewarm,** and **Hot.**

2. To the bowl labeled **Cold,** add 1/2 cup cold milk; to the bowls labeled **Lukewarm** and **None,** add 1/2 cup lukewarm milk; and to the bowl labeled **Hot,** add 1/2 cup hot (not boiled) milk. Stir.

   In which bowl does the junket set most quickly? _____

   After a long time, does the junket get firm in all the bowls? _____

   In which ones doesn't it get firm? _____

☺ Refrigerate. Then gobble up the junket that has set.

★ *Junket contains an enzyme called rennin (rennet) that **denatures**, or breaks down, the protein in milk. The same enzyme is in the stomachs of mammals, including humans. By thickening milk, it keeps milk in the stomach long enough to be digested. The enzyme itself is broken down by heat. The bowl without junket is included as a **control** so you know that it is the junket that is causing the reaction.*

 # Food Imaginings

What makes you feel hungry? Do this when you're not too full or too hungry!

What You Need

- old magazines
- scissors

What You Do

1. From magazines, cut out three pictures of foods that you like and three pictures of foods that you don't like. Mix the pictures up and put them in a pile. Go through the pile quickly and list the foods below in the same order as they are in the pile.

2. Go through the pile again, picking up each picture and looking at it. Imagine taking a bite. Imagine the food in your mouth. Imagine what it tastes like. Try not to move your tongue. Is your mouth watering? A lot or a little? Is your stomach growling? Do you feel hungry, or have you lost your appetite? Write down what you feel. Then go on to the next picture.

Food	How's your mouth?	How's your stomach?

Digestive Decay

Digestion is a dynamic process. This means that the changes it produces happen over time.

What You Need ◆ adult help

- an empty half-gallon milk or juice carton
- masking tape
- scissors
- leftovers from several dinners on different nights
- knife and cutting board
- spoon
- potting soil (or loose dirt)
- wax paper

What You Do

1. Rinse the carton and tape its open end shut. Lay the carton on one side. Then cut a flap in the upper side so you can open it and reach inside.

2. Save some leftovers from dinner. Chop or shred them into small pieces.

3. Spoon the chopped leftovers into the carton and spread them around. Cover with soil.

4. The next day, stir what's in the carton. Add more chopped-up leftovers from this day's dinner. Again, cover with soil. Repeat this for several nights until the carton is almost full.

5. Put the carton where it won't be disturbed or thrown out. Stir the soil every day. Add a spoonful of water if it gets dry.

6. At the end of one week, two weeks, and three weeks, check to see if the soil is done "digesting" the leftovers. To check, stir the mixture and spoon a bit of it onto a piece of wax paper. Examine it. Remember to wash your hands after touching it. Record your findings on the next page.

Digestive Decay

(continued)

Observation	After One Week	After Two Weeks	After Three Weeks
What does it look like?			
Can you see pieces of food?			
What does it smell like?			
What does it feel like?			

When does the mixture look, smell, and feel most like soil? _____

Where did the food go? _____

☺ Use the mixture to fertilize a vegetable garden.
Then gobble up the vegetables that you grow with your compost!

★ *Like digestion, the decay of food in a compost heap depends on chemical reactions. In this case, it's the enzymes secreted by bacteria in the soil that are doing the digesting.*

Thumbs Down

Thumbs have nothing to do with digestion . . . or do they?

What You Need

- peanuts in the shell
- orange
- cheese spread (or peanut butter)
- crackers
- knife
- masking tape

What You Do

1. Lay the food and the knife on the table in front of you.

2. Ask someone to tape your thumbs to your palms so you can't use them.

3. Try to eat each of the foods. Can you get the shell off a peanut? Can you peel the orange? Can you use the knife to spread the cheese? Can you even pick up a cracker?

☺ Gobble up, but don't use your thumbs. Can you do it?

☞ Most other animals don't have thumbs. Some don't even have fingers. Think of how they eat as you figure out ways to solve your problem.

Crunchy Crystals

Have you ever seen ice on a window on a snowy day? Have you ever crunched on rock candy? Have you ever been dazzled by a diamond ring?

All those things are examples of **crystals**. Ice is a crystal of frozen water. Rock candy is a crystal of sugar. Diamonds are crystals of **carbon**, the same substance that makes up coal.

Like everything else, crystals are made up of small parts called **atoms**. What makes crystals so special is that their atoms are lined up in a very orderly pattern. This gives them regular shapes with smooth surfaces and sharp edges. It also makes them hard and very beautiful. Most gems, like diamonds, emeralds, and rubies, are crystals.

Crystals come in many shapes. Some are square boxes. Others look like crooked boxes. Some have six sides instead of four. Some are short and squat; others are long and thin like needles. Their shape depends on the pattern of the atoms inside them, and that depends on what they are made of.

Let's explore the world of crystals. Save the crystals you make in one activity so you can compare them to the crystals you make in other activities. Soon you will have a collection of crystals!

Ice Block

If you could climb inside a crystal of ice, this is what you would see.

What You Need ◆ adult help

- everything you needed in "Molecular Marvels" (page 30)

What You Do

1. Make 12 or more water molecules according to the instructions given in "Molecular Marvels" (page 30). The more the merrier. Push each raisin down so it's in the middle of the toothpick.

2. Working with six molecules, stick one toothpick from each piece of apple into the apple portion of another molecule. This will link the molecules so they make a flat, six-sided shape with six toothpicks sticking up, like in the drawing above. Each piece of apple will have three toothpicks in it.

3. Build another six-sided shape like the first. Add the second shape to the first by sticking each piece of apple in the new layer onto a toothpick that's sticking up from the first layer. Now you have a structure that looks like a cage or the beginning of a tower. Build new layers and add them to your structure. Make it as high or as wide as you want, but don't put more than four toothpicks in each apple.

You have made an ice crystal! Is it firmer than separate water molecules? _____

☺ Use the apples and raisins in an apple tart or popover. Gobble up!

★ *When water freezes into ice, molecules that are next to each other link together through hydrogen atoms, forming hydrogen bonds. Each oxygen atom shares four hydrogen atoms. The bonds in the lattice structure give ice its hardness and rigidity.*

Melon Models

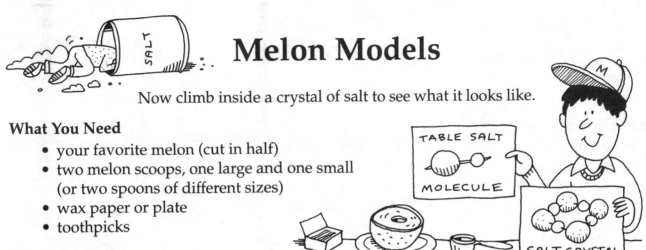

Now climb inside a crystal of salt to see what it looks like.

What You Need

- your favorite melon (cut in half)
- two melon scoops, one large and one small
  (or two spoons of different sizes)
- wax paper or plate
- toothpicks

What You Do

1. Scoop out large and small balls of melon. Stick one large and one small ball on opposite ends of a toothpick. That's a "molecule" of table salt. Make more molecules.

2. To make salt crystal models, stick "molecules" together with toothpicks that join large balls to small balls. Join your molecules so they make a box like the one in the diagram.

Do these models look different from the ones you made in "Ice Block" on page 112?

_____

In what ways? _____

Do you think salt crystals look different from ice crystals?_____

☺ Gobble up the melon balls!

★ _Table salt is made up of one **sodium atom** and one **chlorine atom**. The small melon balls represent the smaller sodium atoms, and the large melon balls represent chlorine atoms. Ice crystals are six-sided structures. Salt crystals are four-sided structures._

Icy Icicles

Look at a cracked ice cube with a magnifying glass. Can you see the crystals?

What You Need ◆ adult help

- newspaper
- piece of window glass (or a mirror)
- 1/2 cup water
- magnifying glass

- 1/3 cup Epsom salt
- food coloring (optional)
- white glue (water soluble)
- stove and small pan

What You Do

1. Spread newspaper over the table. Wash and dry the glass and lay it on the newspaper.

2. Boil the water. Remove it from the heat. Add a few drops of food coloring (if you want colored crystals). Add the Epsom salt and a few drops of glue. Stir until dissolved.

3. Pour some of the mixture over the glass. Lift the edges of newspaper to tilt the glass and spread the mixture around. Then leave the glass alone and watch to see what happens.

4. Store the remaining liquid in a covered container to make more crystals later. Keep the glass with the crystals so you can compare these crystals with others later on.

☹ Don't gobble up these crystals.

As the water dries up, what forms? _____

What shapes do they have? _____

What do they remind you of? _____

★ *Epsom salt makes crystals similar in shape to ice crystals, only they last a lot longer.*

Detecting Differences

Do salt and sugar look alike to you? Can you tell them apart?

What You Need

- salt
- sugar
- piece of black (or dark-colored) paper
- magnifying glass
- two identical glasses
- water
- two teaspoons

What You Do

1. Sprinkle a bit of salt onto one half of the black paper. Keeping the sugar separate from the salt, sprinkle sugar onto the other half.

2. Examine both with the magnifying glass. Do they have different shapes? _____

   What are their shapes? Salt _____ Sugar _____

   Is one bigger than the other? _____ If so, which one? _____

   Are their colors the same? _____ What are their colors? Salt _____ Sugar _____

3. Mix the two together on the paper. Can you tell them apart? _____

4. Fill two glasses to the same height with warm water. Look at them from the side. When the water is clear, add a teaspoon of salt to one and a teaspoon of sugar to the other. Describe any differences you see.

   _____

Salt Shapes

Tired of the tiny crystals in the salt shaker? Here's how to make a big one.

What You Need

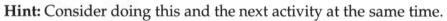

- salt
- water
- measuring cup and tablespoon
- two small bowls
- small piece of aluminum foil
- tweezers
- magnifying glass

Hint: Consider doing this and the next activity at the same time.

What You Do

1. Add two tablespoons of salt to 1/3 cup water. Stir for a few minutes until most of the salt is dissolved. Let it stand for a while so any undissolved salt settles to the bottom.

2. Pour the clear liquid into a bowl. Loosely cover it with foil. Put it aside.

3. After a few days, look into the bowl. What do you see? _____

4. Examine the biggest crystal. What shape is it? _____

5. Make another salt solution (see Step 1) and put it in a clean bowl. Use the tweezers to move the biggest crystal from the first bowl to this new bowl.

6. Repeat these steps to get a huge salt crystal.
   What's the shape of the final crystal? _____

   Is this the same shape you observed for salt in "Detecting Differences" on page 115? _____

☹ Don't gobble up your crystal. Save it to compare to other crystals you make.

★ *As water evaporates, salt molecules come out of solution and join together in crystals.*

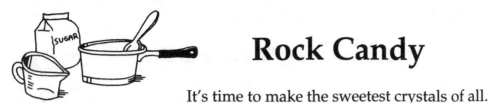

Rock Candy

It's time to make the sweetest crystals of all.

What You Need ◆ adult help

- four pieces of clean cotton string
- four straws
- four paper clips
- one cup water in a large pan
- sugar (about two cups)
- spoon
- four small glasses
- magnifying glass
- stove

What You Do

1. Tie a piece of string around the middle of each straw. Tie a paper clip to the other end of each string.

2. Boil the water. Gradually stir sugar into the boiling water until no more will dissolve. (**Hint:** To make colorful crystals, add food coloring to the water before adding the sugar.)

3. Pour some of the solution into each glass. Lay a straw over the rim of each one so the string and paper clip hangs into the solution. Put the glasses out of the way, but in a place where you can still see them.

4. After a few hours, without touching the glasses, look at the solution and strings with a magnifying glass. What do you see? _____

5. Let the glasses sit for a week or more. Check them once a day or once every other day. Carefully remove any crust that forms on the top of the liquid.

   What is the shape of the crystals that have formed? _____

   Is this the same shape you observed for sugar in "Detecting Differences"? _____

   Why is it important to remove the crust?_____

   ☹ Don't gobble up until you've compared all the crystals you've made.

Food Guide Pyramid Fun

Solve the clues. Then find the sweets in this word search puzzle.

- You put this on pancakes.

_____

- Sometimes you're as slow as this.

_____

- Bees make it and bears love it.

_____

- In a candy box, it's chewy and tan.

_____

- Some people sprinkle this on cereal.

_____

X	T	V	C	U	S	F	R	P	H	Q
M	O	L	A	S	S	E	S	O	H	W
O	A	S	M	U	M	Z	U	K	O	J
L	S	Y	R	D	O	L	G	X	N	T
H	F	R	Q	C	A	R	A	M	E	L
C	A	U	B	F	I	J	R	T	Y	P
N	B	P	X	H	O	H	O	N	F	G
S	U	G	F	U	E	Y	C	Z	W	L

Answers: syrup, molasses, honey, caramel, sugar

Sugar Surprise

When you made "Rock Candy" (page 117), crystals formed from a thick solution of sugar that was allowed to *evaporate*, or dry up. Do you think all sugary liquids will form crystals?

What You Need   ◆ adult help

- three or more: milk, molasses, honey, maple syrup, corn syrup, or caramel sauce
- spoons
- baking pan
- clock
- oven

What You Do

1. Turn the oven on low (warm). Using a clean spoon for each liquid, put one spoonful of each liquid on the pan. Be careful. Don't let them run into one another.

2. Put the pan in the oven. Every half hour, check the liquids. Take the pan out when all of them are dry. Did each liquid make crystals? Record your answers below.

3. Examine the crystals that were made. What are their shapes? Record your results.

Liquid	Crystals?	Shape?

★ *Sugar solutions may not always crystallize, either because they're not made from a single kind of sugar or because the sugar absorbs moisture from the air and thus stays in solution.*

Icy Ice Cream

Have you ever eaten ice cream that had chunks of ice in it? Did you like it?

What You Need

- large spoon
- one pint smooth (no chips or nuts) ice cream
- two bowls (one labeled **Gel**)
- freezer
- one teaspoon unflavored gelatin
- measuring spoons
- water

What You Do

1. Spoon equal amounts of ice cream into two bowls. Let the ice cream melt, then refreeze both bowls of ice cream. Let the ice cream melt again. Then refreeze. Do this again and again until you can see and taste ice crystals in the ice cream.

2. Take the bowls out one last time. While the ice cream is melting, make the gelatin. Mix one teaspoon of gelatin with $1^1/_2$ tablespoons of water. When the gelatin is soft, add $1^1/_2$ tablespoons of very hot water. Stir well. Pour the gelatin into the bowl labeled **Gel**. Stir.

4. Mix three tablespoons of water into the other bowl (to make the amounts even).

5. Put both bowls in the freezer.

6. When the ice cream is frozen, remove the bowls. Look, feel, and taste the ice cream.

   Do you see ice crystals in both? _____ Does one feel gritty? _____

   Which one tastes smoother? _____

   ☞ Gelatin keeps water from freezing into large ice crystals. It's an *emulsifier* (see "All Mixed Up," page 56). Read the labels on ice cream containers. Which ingredient is the emulsifier?

Cool Glass

Did you ever wonder why your parents' best drinking glasses are called crystal?

What You Need   ◆ adult help

- butter or margarine
- one cup sugar
- cookie sheet
- refrigerator
- frying pan
- stove
- wooden spoon

What You Do

1. Grease a cookie sheet with the butter or margarine and put it in the refrigerator.

2. Put the sugar in the pan. Heat it on medium, stirring all the time. Be patient.

3. As soon as the sugar melts into a golden brown liquid, take the cookie sheet out of the refrigerator. Quickly pour the sugary liquid onto the sheet. Tilt the sheet to spread the liquid. What happens? _____

4. Break off a piece. Hold it up to a light. Can you see through it? _____

   Do you see any crystals? _____ Taste it. Is it sweet? _____

☺ Use bits of your "glass" to decorate cakes or cookies and then gobble them up!

☞ You just made sugar glass in the same way that people make real glass. It's hard to believe, but glass is made of melted sand instead of sugar. After the sand is melted, it's cooled so quickly that crystals don't have time to form. Remember how long it took you to make crystals in "Salt Shapes" (page 116) and "Rock Candy" (page 117)? If you had put the solutions in the refrigerator, the salt and sugar would not have made large crystals.

Crazy Caramel

Can you take the sweetness out of sugar?

What You Need ◆ adult help

- one cup sugar
- two small frying pans
- wooden spoon
- stove
- measuring cup
- hot water
- two coffee cups

What You Do

1. Put the sugar in one frying pan. Stir it over medium heat. Keep stirring. Be patient.
2. As soon as the sugar melts into a golden brown liquid, remove it from the heat. Pour half of the liquid into the other pan.
3. Very slowly pour 1/2 cup hot water into the first pan. Be careful! It may splatter.
4. Put this pan back on the burner. Stir until the liquid is smooth. Pour it into a cup. Let it cool.
5. Put the second pan on the burner. Stir until the sugar becomes a dark brown liquid. Then, as before, take it off the burner and carefully add 1/2 cup hot water. Reheat the liquid and pour it into a cup to cool.
6. When both syrups are cool, taste them. Taste sugar. List the three in the order of sweetness, with the sweetest first. 1st _____ 2nd _____ 3rd _____

   What do you think happened to the sweetness? _____
   (Think about what you learned about chemical changes from the activities in "Riveting Reactions," beginning on page 64.)

★ *Extreme heat breaks down sugar's crystalline structure and takes away its sweetness.*

Earthly Eats

Earth is an amazing planet. It gives us all the things we need to live—from the air
we breathe to the soil we grow our food in, from the water we drink to the materials we use
to build our homes. Earth is the only place like this
in the solar system—and maybe in the whole universe.

How did Earth get to be like it is? How did mountains get to be so big?
Why does the ground shake and quake? Why do rivers twist and turn?
You won't get the answers to all of your questions in the following activities,
but you'll make a start.

The most important thing to remember about Earth is that it is always changing.
Does that surprise you? After all, your home stays in the same place day after day.
Your school doesn't move. The playground is where it was yesterday.

While that's all true, Earth is still changing. It's just that the changes that happen are usually
too small to notice from one day to the next. You can't tell when a bit of soil in your garden has
washed away in an overnight shower, but if there were heavy rains and a flood,
you would certainly notice. Changes to Earth can be large or small.

Changes that happened in the past made Earth what it is today. Changes that happen today
will reshape Earth for tomorrow. Clues about how these changes work
lie in the rocks and dirt and also deep inside Earth.

Earth Egg

How is an egg like Earth? You'll find out.

What You Need   ◆ adult help

- globe or picture of Earth
- one unpeeled, hard-boiled egg
- brown and blue water-based markers
- knife and cutting board

What You Do

1. Color an egg to make it look like Earth. Use brown for land and blue for oceans.

2. Carefully cut your egg in half across the middle.

3. Look at the cut surface (or cross-section) of the egg. Name the three layers you see.

Earth is made of three layers, too. We live on the rocky surface called the **crust**. The crust goes all around Earth, even under the oceans. Below the crust is the layer called the **mantle**. It, too, is solid. In the middle of Earth is the **core**. It has a liquid outside and a solid inside. Pretend your egg is Earth. Which part of the egg is the crust? the mantle? the core? Draw a picture of the cut surface, or cross-section, of your egg. Label these parts.

☺ Peel and gobble up your Earth—oops—your egg!

Broken Earth

Here's another way an egg is like Earth.

What You Need

- globe or picture of Earth
- one unpeeled, hard-boiled egg
- brown, blue, and black water-based markers

What You Do

1. Draw Earth on an egg. Use brown for land and blue for oceans.

2. Gently roll or tap the egg on the table to make some cracks in the shell. Don't crush the shell and don't pick at the cracks! Trace the cracks with the black marker.

   Are any of the cracks on land? _____ in an ocean? _____

   Do pieces of shell fall off? _____

3. Hold the egg at each end with the fingers of both hands. Twist the egg. You've just created an eggquake! Do the cracks get larger? _____

   Does the shell break where there are no cracks? _____

   Do pieces of shell fall off? _____

   ☺ Peel and wash your egg, then gobble up!

★ *Like the cracked egg, Earth's crust, together with the outer portion of the mantle, is made up of large pieces called **plates**. The plates are in constant motion. **Fault lines** are where two plates meet. Faults behave like the cracks in the egg. When a lot of force is put on them, they move suddenly and cause an earthquake.*

Mount Sandwich

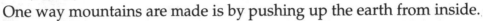

One way mountains are made is by pushing up the earth from inside.

What You Need

- three slices of bread
- peanut butter or cream cheese
- jam
- knife

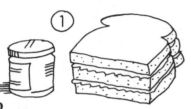

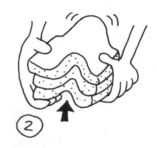

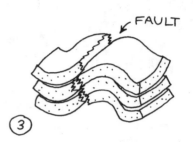

What You Do

1. Spread peanut butter or cream cheese on one slice of bread. Put a second slice on top. Cover that with your favorite jam. Put a third slice on top. Don't cut your sandwich.

2. Pick the sandwich up with both hands, one on either side, with your fingers on the bottom and your thumbs on top. Make a mountain by pushing up the middle with your fingers. Now make a valley by pushing down in the middle with your thumbs. What happened to the bread in each case?

3. To make a mountain with a fault in it, push your sandwich up in the middle as in Step 2. Lay one side of the mountain down onto the bread. You have created a fault. An earthquake could happen here.

4. Cut your sandwich in half to make two rectangles. Hold the two halves so they touch. Slide one half up and one half down. Then slide the halves back and forth. Earth's crust moves along faults in both these ways. When the movement is very sudden, there is an earthquake.

☺ Gobble up your mountain of a sandwich!

Pudding Power

Why does Earth's crust move?

What You Need ◆ adult help

- one package chocolate pudding mix (not instant)
- milk
- pot (glass if possible)
- stove
- large spoon
- confectioners' sugar
- pie plate

What You Do

1. Make the chocolate pudding according to the instructions on the box. When the pudding comes to a boil, turn the burner to low and stop stirring, but leave the pudding on the burner.

2. Lightly sprinkle sugar on top. Watch where the sugar goes.

3. Pour the pudding into the pie plate. Let it cool uncovered.

   What happens to the pudding's surface? _____

   What would these be called on Earth? _____

☺ Gobble up!

★ *When a liquid is heated from below, the hot part rises to the top where it cools off. Then it sinks. This makes a circular motion. Inside Earth it is very hot, creating a lot of **turbulence**, or intense motion, that in turn moves the crust (the sugar). The cracks in the cooled pudding are like faults. Through faults on Earth, the hot melted rocks in Earth's mantle ooze out or **erupt** (burst forth) in the form of volcanoes.*

Hot Stuff

Design your own experiment. Think of a way to make a volcano that can be eaten after it blows up. (**Hint:** Look back at "Fizzing Fun" on page 68 and "Fizzing Power" on page 70.) Do those activities give you an idea for making your volcano erupt? What will you use to build the volcano? Remember, you have to eat it afterwards. When you've come up with a plan, write down what you need and what you will do. Then do it!

What You Need

-
-
-
-
-

What You Do

1. _____

   _____

2. _____

   _____

3. _____

   _____

4. _____

   _____

5. _____

   _____

Hot Stuff

(continued)

Use this page to write down how your experiment worked
and to draw a picture of the volcano you built.

_____

_____

_____

_____

_____

Land of Oats

A bowl of oatmeal is good for you. Here's how it can also be fun!

What You Need ◆ adult help

- oatmeal (instant or regular)
- milk
- honey
- cinnamon
- raisins
- water
- spoon
- bowl
- pan
- stove

What You Do

1. Make oatmeal as directed on the package, using less water than called for to make it thick. Fill a bowl halfway. (**Hint:** To make a landscape that will last, use clay made from $2^{1}/_{2}$ parts flour, one part salt, and one part water.)

2. With a spoon, carve a landscape in the oatmeal. Make mountains and valleys. Put in a winding river leading from a mountain top to the sea.

3. Fill your river by dripping milk or honey into it from the top of the hill. Watch how it runs down the hill. Use the cinnamon for soil.

4. Try other things. What happens to your river if you dam it up with raisins? What happens to the soil when there's a flood?

☺ Gobble up!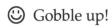

Cinnamon Sediments

What happens to the land when a stream of water carries dirt away?

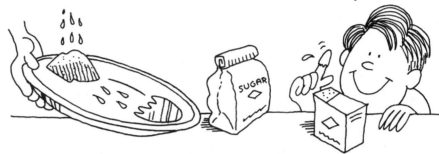

What You Need

- sugar
- cinnamon
- measuring spoons
- large plate
- water

What You Do

1. Mix one teaspoon sugar and 1/2 teaspoon cinnamon on the plate. Pile it on one side.

2. Holding the plate on a slight tilt, drip water over the pile. Pretend the pile is a hill of dirt and the water is rain. What happens to the hill? _____

   Where does the dirt go? _____ Taste to make sure.

   What happens to the rainwater? _____

3. Let the water dry with the plate on a tilt.

   Does the new landscape look the same as the one you started with? _____

   Did anything disappear? Do you have the same amount of sugar, cinnamon, and water that you started with? _____ Is it in another form? _____

☺ Mix soft butter with the sugar and cinnamon. Spread on toast. Gobble up!

★ *Rain changes Earth. It washes dirt into streams that carry it to rivers that in turn carry it to oceans. There the dirt settles, forming new land. Moving dirt around like this is called* **erosion**. *The next time it rains, look for examples of erosion.*

Pressed Rocks

Find a rock that has layers. It is called a *sedimentary* rock.

What You Need   ◆ adult help

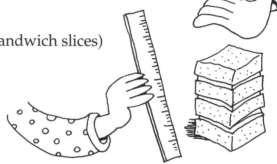

- one slice of soft white or wheat bread
- one square cheese slice (from packaged sandwich slices)
- butter
- ruler
- knife and cutting board
- stove and frying pan

What You Do

1. Cut the crusts off the bread. Cut each slice into four equal pieces. Cut the cheese slice into quarters. Pile up four pieces of bread, one on top of another. Put a piece of cheese in between each piece of bread. (You'll have one piece of cheese left over.)

2. Measure the height of the sandwich and record the measurement. Height: _____

3. With the palm of your hand, press down on the sandwich for a minute and then let go. Measure and record its height. Height after pressing: _____

4. Put a pat of butter in the frying pan and grill your cheese sandwich.

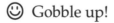

☺ Gobble up!

☞ In Step 3, you made a sedimentary, or layered, rock. Sedimentary rock is made by pressure. Heat turns it into another kind of rock, called *metamorphic*.
Think about how your "rock" changed in Step 4.

Pop Rocks

Sedimentary rocks don't always have flat layers. Sometimes they look all mixed up.

What You Need ◆ adult help

- six to eight cups popped popcorn
- two to three cups crispy rice cereal
- one cup chopped nuts
- three tablespoons butter
- 1/2 cup brown sugar
- two tablespoons maple syrup
- large mixing bowl
- stove and small pan

What You Do

1. In the bowl, mix the popcorn, cereal, and nuts.

2. Melt the butter in the pan. Add the sugar and stir until it melts. Remove from the heat. Add the maple syrup. Pour the mixture over the popcorn mixture. Stir.

3. While it is still warm and gooey, pick up globs of the mixture. Press into balls.

   How do these "rocks" look different from the ones in "Pressed Rocks" on page 132?

☺ Gobble up!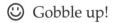

☞ You just made a kind of sedimentary rock called *conglomerate*.
That means it has large pebbles and other pieces of rock stuck together
by mud that acts like glue. Go outside. Can you find examples of conglomerate rock?

Food Guide Pyramid Fun

You're in an underground mine, but you're not searching for gold or silver.
You're trying to find a way to a balanced meal.

Feasting on Fossils

When animals and plants die and get covered in layers of dirt,
they leave marks in the rocks that are formed over time. These marks are called *fossils*.

What You Need

- graham crackers
- large, sealable plastic bag
- clear glass pie plate
  (or clear glass baking dish)
- large spoon
- "fossils": animal crackers,
  gummy dinosaurs, raisins,
  nuts, small pretzels, etc.
- bowl of prepared pudding
- whipped topping
- refrigerator

What You Do

1. Put the graham crackers in the bag. Crush them by pounding with your fist.

2. On the bottom of the pie plate, put a layer of cracker crumbs. Sprinkle a few fossils around. Spoon on a layer of pudding and add a few more fossils. Then spread a layer of whipped topping and add more fossils.

3. Repeat, adding at least one more layer of cracker crumbs, pudding, and topping. Don't forget to add a few more fossils between each layer. Refrigerate for one or more hours.

   Look at your layers from the side. How many layers did you make? _____

   ☺ Search for fossils as you gobble up the pudding.
How many can you find?

135

My *Gobble Up Science* Review

1. My favorite activity was _____

2. I liked it the best because _____

3. My least favorite activity was _____

4. I didn't like it because _____

5. I had the most fun doing _____

6. I made the biggest mess doing _____

7. I liked gobbling up _____

8. I didn't like gobbling up _____

9. I liked learning how to use _____

10. I would like to do more activities about _____

Please send your review to:
The Learning Works
P.O. Box 6187
Santa Barbara, CA 93160